Making & Flying
STUNT KITES
& One-Liners

Wolfgang Schimmelpfennig

Sterling Publishing Co., Inc.
New York

Credits
Title page photo: Wolfgang Schimmelpfennig, Hamburg
Photos:
Pages 13, 14, 17, 18: G. P. Reichelt
All others: by the author
Drawings:
Pages 15, 16, 75, 78, 79: Bernhard Maas, Hamburg
All others: Peter Morgenbrodt

Translated by Elisabeth E. Reinersmann
Edited by Claire Bazinet

Library of Congress Cataloging-in-Publication Data

Schimmelpfennig, Wolfgang.
    Making and flying stunt kites and one-liners / by Wolfgang
Schimmelpfennig; [translated by Elisabeth E. Reinersmann].
        p. cm.
    Abridgement of Lenkdrachen and Neue Lenkdrachen und
Einleiner.
    Includes index.
    ISBN 0-8069-0870-X
    1. Kites. I. Schimmelpfennig, Wolfgang. Lenkdrachen.
II. Schimmelpfennig, Wolfgang. Neue Lenkdrachen und
Einleiner. III. Title.
TL759.6.S78S34 1995
629.133′32—dc20   95-20180
                                                CIP

10 9 8 7 6 5 4 3 2 1

First paperback edition published in 1996 by
Sterling Publishing Company, Inc.
387 Park Avenue South, New York, N.Y. 10016
This volume is an abridgement of two volumes
originally published by Falken-Verlag GmbH, Niedernhausen/Ts.
Lenkdrachen bauen und fliegen © 1989/92 by Falken-Verlag GmbH,
Niedernhausen/Ts. and *Neue Lenkdrachen und Einleiner bauen und
    fliegen*
© 1993 by Falken-Verlag GmbH, Niedernhausen/Ts.
English translation © 1995 by Sterling Publishing Co., Inc.
Distributed in Canada by Sterling Publishing
c/o Canadian Manda Group, One Atlantic Avenue, Suite 105
Toronto, Ontario, Canada M6K 3E7
Distributed in Great Britain and Europe by Cassell PLC
Wellington House, 125 Strand, London WC2R 0BB, England
Distributed in Australia by Capricorn Link (Australia) Pty Ltd.
P.O. Box 6651, Baulkham Hills, Business Centre, NSW 2153,
    Australia
Printed and bound in Hong Kong
All rights reserved

Sterling ISBN 0-8069-0870-X Trade
            0-8069-0871-8 Paper

Contents

Introduction

The sky has long held special fascination, prompting some individuals, as early as the fifteenth century, to dangle below pyramid-shaped structures high in the air. Others, since the kite's inception in China about 2,000 years ago, were content to gaze upwards.

Over the years, the popularity of kite flying has fluctuated. The development of the maneuverable kite, in the mid-1970s, and the subsequent availability of new, kite-making materials have had a great deal to do with the current boom. Steered with two lines, stunt kites can perform amazing maneuvers and, with the new materials and construction techniques, speeds of up to 125 miles (200 km) per hour are not unusual.

Flying a stunt kite is not difficult. With the technique of steering quickly mastered, you'll soon be performing magical flight patterns in the sky. The enjoyment is that much greater if the kite is one you designed and built yourself.

Although people usually think first of constructing a stunt kite, having seen the astounding maneuvers these kites can perform, those same kite builders soon discover how much fun it is to see a handcrafted, single-line kite soaring steadily high in the air, looking as if it is "nailed" to the sky. These kites do not impress for their speed and movement, but for their esthetic beauty. It is here that kite builders discover the artist in themselves, playing with shapes and color and, in the process, creating truly fantastic kites.

This book is meant to provide both inspiration and practical advice. The kites presented cover a wide variety. Some are fast, some have intricate designs, and some exert a great deal of pulling power: in other words, a kite for every taste. For best results, take your own abilities into consideration when choosing your project. All the kites have also been designed to avoid unnecessary "noise pollution," and some of the single-line kites feature new design elements that add interest to the sport of kite-flying.

I would like to thank all who have contributed to this book. My special thanks to Peter Morgenbrodt, who, with a great deal of enthusiasm, created the extraordinary step-by-step illustrations.

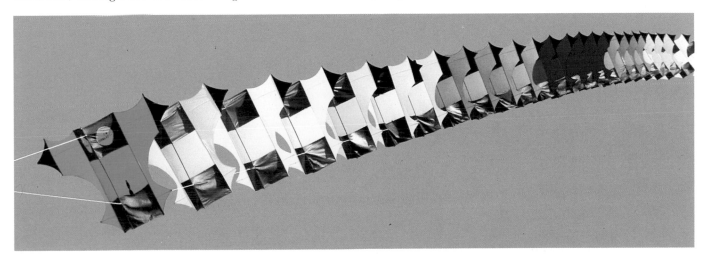

Creative Kite Designs

Kite-flying competitions are where you will find the most beautiful kites, in all designs and color combinations. Artists the world over create these flying objects, often inspiring spectators to try a hand in kite building and learn the secrets of shape and color. Once the building techniques are mastered, ideas can quickly become reality.

The kite shown below, built by noted kite maker Donald Collado of Hawaii, called "Bird of Paradise" shows a harmonious use of color and shapes. Collado's designs are excellent examples of variety in kite making.

Here are some suggestions for making artistically exceptional kites. Be creative in the designing and building of your kite and the result will be unmistakably original. Your own imaginative ideas about color combinations, design, and shape—in short, your own creative labors—will be translated into a flying "composition," with immensely pleasing results.

A new kite idea begins long before the actual building, or even a drawing of the planned design is put on paper. Emotions and imagination play a vital role. Important ideas might surface while you are looking through magazines and brochures, or while meeting and talking with other people. They should all be carefully recorded. Design ideas come in many small, individual increments; and never in sequence. For that reason, it is important to keep notes, especially with regard to color and shapes. Few successful kite builders are

ever found without their notebook. Make sketches of everything that might be important to a design that interests you. You may never use an idea, but it doesn't matter. Sometimes, it can take years before you incorporate an idea you once sketched.

Before you actually start working up a design, think about these questions:

1. What effect do I want to achieve? What kind of reaction do I want from spectators? Will I want to fly my kite by night? Should the kite stand out because of its bright colors, or should it have a more moderate design?

2. What should be the shape of the kite: square, rectangular, boxlike? The shape is often determined by the motif you have chosen; too, you might want to chain several kites together.

3. How much room do I need for a particular design? A parafoil with a keel, for instance, has only a limited amount of space for an intricate pattern.

4. What size kite do I want? The problem of transporting the kite is a major concern in size, but the visual representation you have in mind will also influence your decision. Many designs can become no more than a blur when the kite is flying high in the sky. For complex designs, you need a kite that spans at least 4 yards (3½ metres).

5. How much will it cost? Large kites often can't be built inexpensively; sometimes you need several square yards of nylon sailcloth. Always keep in mind that there will surely be some waste and the fact that larger kites always need graphite rods.

6. What material will I use? Nylon sailcloth comes in many different grades. The most important factors are weight and elasticity. While you need elasticity for a parafoil, a stunt kite must be made from a very strong nylon. Spars don't necessarily have to be made of graphite. Wood spars often will do just fine. Even a very complicated kite can be made using wood. The box kite below, made by kite artist Peter Malinski of Bremen, Germany, was made with wooden spars. Replacing a broken strut quickly is no problem for Peter.

7. Do I want to sew the kite? Sewing a particular design is not always possible. Limits are often imposed by the fact that only a few kite builders are also experienced tailors. Be realistic when evaluating your skills. If you should come across a particular problem, kite shops are only too willing to help.

8. How much time do I have for the project? Some complex designs could take several months to complete. If kite building is a hobby, you will want to spend time on it in relation to other activities. More extensive work should only be attempted after you have gained experience, particularly with regard to the use of a sewing machine.

Color

The world of color is endless. People can perceive over ten thousand different shades. Of course, when it comes to nylon sailcloth, the choice of color is not nearly so large. But it is important to understand the suitability and impact of colors before choosing them.

Scientists have established theories about combining colors. Goethe recognized the connections between harmonizing colors and developed a color circle that remains, to this day, an important tool for artists. Color harmonies and combinations, however, are not dogma. Not so long ago, for example, blue and green were considered incompatible.

Experiment with colors by using small pieces of paper in different color combinations. Colors opposite each other on the color wheel, considered complementary, create strong contrasts yet remain in harmony with one another. A "colorless" color, such as grey, white, and black, is the result of mixing complementary colors, but not all the colors considered opposites create colorless colors. Some combinations (maybe three or more different colors) equally removed from each other on the color wheel might have the same result. In other words, not only are complementary colors considered harmonious, but so, too, are those colors similarly removed from one another.

Effect of Colors

You might think that color and shape have little to do with one other, but it is well known that a red car can be detected more quickly than a white one. People who make warning and directional signs have long taken color into consideration. It should also be taken into account when designing a

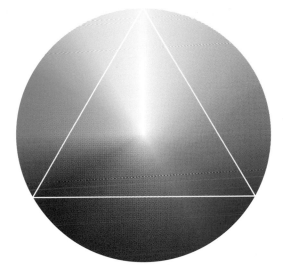

kite, so as to have the desired effect. The color influences may be physical as well as psychological in nature. In general, we see the different colors as:

yellow	movement, lively, stimulating, joyful
orange	active, invigorating, sour, garish, autumnal, organic
red	speed, enthusiasm, loudness, heat, very stimulating
violet	passive and calming, deep, dark
blue	concentration
green	fresh, balancing, very calming

Black and white are not considered colors in the true sense. However, white is seen as expressing purity and clarity, while black is considered powerful, dark, and heavy.

Color and Space

Colors are able to make an object appear either smaller or larger, light or heavy, prominent or remote. Keep in mind the effect that colors have when you design your kite.

The general rule is that shapes painted on a flat surface, using lighter colors, seem to be positioned more in the foreground, while shapes in darker colors exist in the background. The rule is reversed for three-dimensional objects: dark surfaces seem to be closer, while lighter surfaces seem farther away.

Russian artist Wassily Kandinsky (1866–1944) has given shapes an inner quality: some shapes underscore the effect of a color while others diminish it. If a triangle is painted yellow, a square green, and a circle blue, the effects are highlighted. Certain colors, like yellow, green, or orange, become more lively when used in pointed shapes. Others, like blue and black, are intensified when used for round shapes.

The brothers Romeo and Donald Collado show a deep understanding of the effects of colors in relation to depth of space. The light-colored sailboats in "Bird of Paradise" (see page 4) spring into the foreground, while the dark color of the sky seems to deepen the background.

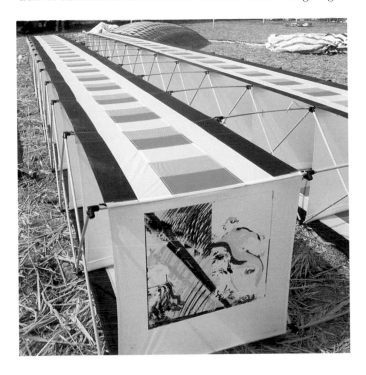

Designing Shapes

Shapes give an object its distinct form. The most simple shape in a design is the dot. In spite of its simplicity, a dot fulfills an important function. A dot draws the viewer's eye towards a certain spot on the sail. Several dots arranged in a row can form a line that, again, draws the eye to a particular point (A). We distinguish between constructed and free lines. While constructed lines follow a plan (B), lines drawn freehand (C) convey a free-flowing rhythm.

When drawing lines, remember that thin lines appear to be longer, while thick lines seem to be shorter (D). We also distinguish between kinds of lines. Straight lines appear solid and static. Angled lines appear hard and unyielding (E). Bent lines appear soft and friendly (F).

The direction of a line is also important. Again, we distinguish between different orientations: upward lines appear to be soaring and active (G). They can be used to express pride and to get attention. Vertical lines (H) convey quietness and composure. They mark the horizon and convey stability. A diagonal line expresses movement and brings life to the scene (I). For the right-handed person, this line moves upwards to the right and descends to the left.

Creating Shapes and Space on a Surface

When creating a kite, one is generally restricted to two dimensions. If you want to produce a three-dimensional shape, you must take additional rules into account. The illusion of spatial depth can be created by two apparently different planes: the foreground and the background. Making shapes smaller or larger creates the impression of distance and nearness: an object appears smaller the farther away it is from us (A). This impression is reinforced by letting shapes overlap and gradually drawing them smaller (B). Lines that do not proceed parallel to the edges seem to retreat into the distance (C). Spatial depth is also created by making individual planes smaller and moving them closer together (D).

Three-dimensional effects are also supported by contrasts. As mentioned previously, lighter surfaces appear to be closer, while darker surfaces move towards the back. Accordingly, light/shadow effects are also a means of creating spatial effects. For instance, light falling on a surface at an angle can, if drawn correctly, make a surface appear to be an object. Besides black and white, areas painted in shades of gray also play a role in such designs and are often used to create background (E, F, G, H, I).

Ideas for Kite Designs

Every kite with an interesting design will attract the attention of spectators. Donald Collado has said that the best piece of art is the one that moves the eyes of the beholder across the artwork with emotional and esthetic involvement.

How can an artist achieve such results? In addition to the rules of design already discussed, the positioning of a figure on the kite is important. It is not always necessary to center the figure or object. A certain interesting tension can be created by placing the important part of the design off-center, at the edge of the kite. Such asymmetry can lend interesting dynamics to a design.

Ideas and inspiration for original designs are everywhere. You will never be at a loss for creative ideas if you keep your eyes and ears open.

6

Materials and Techniques

Kite Coverings

Improvements in sail material are mainly responsible for the rapid and continuing development of kites. A rugged and, at the same time, lightweight material first became available with the introduction of nylon sailcloth (ripstop nylon).

Nylon kite coverings are widely available in weights of ½ to 1½ ounce per square yard (20 to 60 grams per square metre), and also in different degrees of flexibility. While parafoils are commonly built using stretchable material, a less elastic material is preferred for building a stunt kite. The seams of a parafoil are exposed to a tremendous amount of stress; if stretched too much, as during intense wind gusts, the material can tear at the seams. Stunt kites, on the other hand, are made more durable by reinforcing the cutting edges with Dacron binding. The result then is a particularly stiff sail which increases the flying speed of the kite; in addition, it reduces the tendency of the trailing edge to flutter.

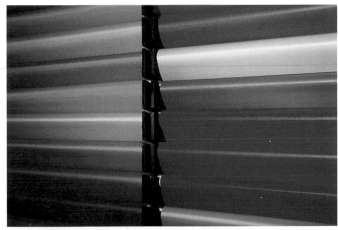
Nylon sailcloth is available in many different colors.

Many different spar materials are on the market.

Sails for stunt kites that are even faster are made with Mylar film. While this material hardly stretches at all, it is difficult to work with because it has a tendency to crease. Stunt kite specialists also like to use polyester for the sail. This material has little give, is easy to work with, is particularly resistant to stretching, and has excellent water-repellent qualities. Nylon and other sailcloths are available in many different colors and qualities. It is not always necessary to buy the most expensive. If, however, the material will be subjected to extreme stress, it is advisable not to use second-grade nylon. The photo (upper left) shows some of the many colors of nylon sailcloth available. Make sure you pay attention to the grain of the fabric when cutting out the sails. Nylon sailcloth always has to be sewn.

For covering the frame of a kite that is not exposed to high speed and high tension, you might also look to a plastic covering called Tyvek. This paperlike material has distinguished itself by its light weight and resistance to tearing. It is inexpensive yet durable.

Framing Materials

The composition of spar material plays a significant role in the aerodynamics of your kite.

Wood and Bamboo

Wood and bamboo work well for constructing the frame of a kite. In Asia, traditional kite builders still use bamboo, either round or split. In order to be able to properly split and use bamboo, the shoot should be at least 1¼ inches (3–4 cm) in diameter. Specialists use bamboo that is closer to 2 inches (5 cm) thick. Since bamboo shoots of this size are often difficult to obtain, already split bamboo rods are used almost exclusively to make traditional Asian kites.

Whole bamboo rods can also be used. With some exceptions, they make fine and affordable frames for larger kites. One needs to be careful when choosing bamboo rods so as not to upset the symmetry of the frame. Disadvantages are the bamboo's relatively high weight, and the fact that, because bamboo is by nature less even, balancing the frame might be difficult. Too, should bamboo become bent, it will not return to its original shape.

Other affordable materials, such as birch and ramin wood, should not be ignored. The huge box kite illustrated on page 5 is an example of how wood can still be used in these times of modern materials. It also makes it easy to replace a broken strut, which does happen now and then. People often build a prototype, using less expensive wood for the frame. Later, after the design has passed all flying tests, the wood can be replaced with a more expensive material. The frame for a stunt kite should only be made with round wooden dowels.

Aluminum

Traditional aluminum works less well for kite frames because of its weight and tendency to deform. Use only connectors made from this material. Arrow shafts, traditionally used in archery, are made from an aluminum alloy of high quality. This material is particularly good for tetrahedron kites, like those that were made by Alexander Graham Bell. However, the huge cost involved usually makes one look for a less expensive material.

Fibreglass-Reinforced Plastic

Tubes made of this material come in every conceivable size and are ordinarily used for building oversized, huge kites, where the diameter of the tubes is from ½ to close to 1 inch (1.2 to 2.2 cm). To attach accessories, such as stand-offs, sail-mountings, and other devices that are decorative rather than a means of getting the kite into the air, kite builders prefer narrower tubes close to ⅛ inch (0.3 cm). Because of the disadvantages of high flexibility and weight, fibreglass-reinforced plastic is used only on a limited basis for modern kite frames.

NOTE: Care must be taken when cutting this and other synthetic materials. A fibreglass splinter can penetrate the skin easily, and the dust caused by smoothing cut ends by sanding is hazardous; it should not be inhaled. Use of gloves, protective eye covering, and filter mask are strongly recommended.

Epoxy

Used in archery and model building, tubes made of epoxy-reinforced fibreglass are also ideal for kite building, providing speed and stability for a flawless flight. Lighter and stronger than fibreglass-reinforced plastic tubing, epoxy tubes are filament-wound on the inside and fibreglass-reinforced on the outside. This process adds stiffness. Epoxy tubes can be bought in various diameters and in lengths from about 32 to 54 inches (82–137 cm). If longer rods are needed, they can be connected by using sleeves.

Also available are epoxy hollow-rod systems. The pieces are connected with quick-drying glue halfway into the end of each rod. The rod that is to be connected is then fixed over the other end of the sleeve. Kite builders with ingenuity and skill slip a section of rubber into the inside of the sleeve that is connecting two rods, adding a safety-ball to the end of the rods. If the spar is taken apart, the separate sections will always return to their proper places when reassembled.

Graphite

Graphite is one of the newest building materials on the market. Rods made from graphite are lightweight and stiff and can be used in many ways to build frames. Because of their extraordinary resistance to distortion, solid graphite rods are particularly useful in constructing stunt kites.

Rods made of graphite come in diameters of about ⅛ inch (0.2–0.3 cm), but graphite tubes are available in many sizes. This material withstands extraordinary stress and is almost unbreakable. If, however, a rod or tube should break, utmost care is called for. Splintered graphite is very sharp; it can easily pierce the skin and is difficult to remove. The dust created when cutting, also, must not be inhaled. Nocks, available in many different sizes, can be matched easily to different-size graphite rods. If the diameter of a rod is very large, the nocks are attached to the rod end with the help of an aluminum tip. For thinner rods, so-called "fit-over" nocks can be attached directly to the end of the rod.

PVC Tubes

Now, as in the past, connectors made from PVC tubes are

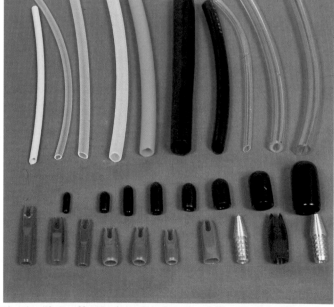

Plastic tubes effectively connect rods while arrow nocks and elastic cord are used for sail tension.

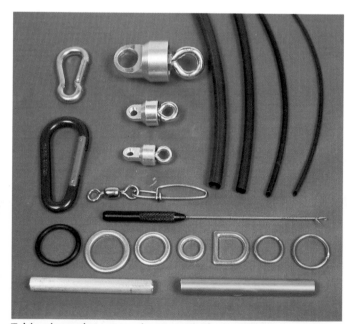

Tubing is used to secure knots; swivels, snap-links, as well as loops and hooks, are indispensable to connect kite lines.

most often used and represent an affordable solution. PVC tubes are available in different sizes and strengths (see page 8). Thin, clear tubes can even be used, in some cases, to support part of the frame.

Connecting Techniques

During the last few years, materials have changed greatly and so have the techniques used to build kites. In the past, wood and bamboo rods were tied together in cross-over fashion, but the kite industry today has made available a number of different and complex connecting devices made from such materials as hard-PVC, Ertalon, PUR, and rubber. In Asia, kite rods are still connected the old-fashioned way, by lashing them together. One big disadvantage is that these kites are difficult to disassemble, which is why the wonderful, huge kites made in Bali are never seen in other countries. Kite builders living in the West have it much easier. The huge star kite (below left), which measures over five yards (4½ metres) in diameter, when dismantled can be reduced to a compact package less than five feet (two metres) in length.

The availability of high-tech connectors has also set new standards for the stunt kite builder. The Scanner (page 38), with the rudder added to the end of the keel and its frame made of graphite rods, is one example of how modern material can be used. As is the case with every kite presented in this book, all intersection and T-connectors are, for the most part, made from tubes according to conventional methods. However, such connectors are easily interchangeable with those shown in the photo at right (top), primarily used for stunt kites:

1. T-connector for the tip of the kite
2. Intersection connector for V-shaped kites
3. Intersection connector for profile kites
4. Lateral bar and strut connector
5. Notched end caps

These accessories make kite building a lot easier. They are lightweight, easy to work with, and add to a kite's flying capabilities. However, connectors made from ordinary tubes have their place; they are less expensive and easier to obtain. Working with them, on the other hand, is slightly more difficult as they have to be secured either with tape or fast-acting glue.

The photo below (bottom) shows some of the many single-line connectors available on the market:

1. Intersection connector for tetrahedron kite
2. Various sizes of center connectors for star-shaped kites
3. End caps
4. Slotted end caps
5. V-connector for Eddy kites

Some of the connectors available in kite shops, to be used in stunt kite construction.

Connectors for the frame of this box kite were handcrafted from hard fibreglass plastic.

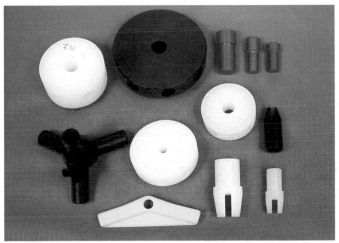

Individual connectors for single-line kites can be made from hard plastic.

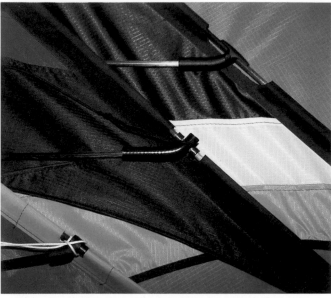

Modern T-connectors that won't slip when used with lateral bar connectors make frame building much easier.

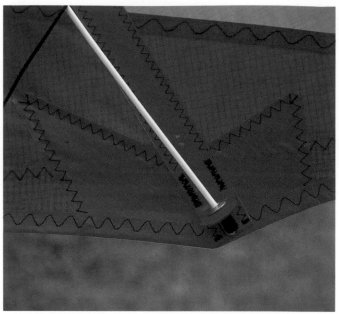

For stand-offs, find a secure place at the trailing edge.

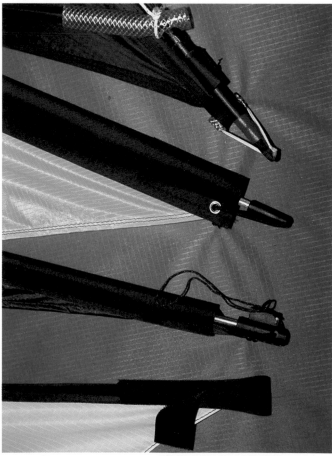

To properly stretch the sail's pockets, the stretchers must be adjustable.

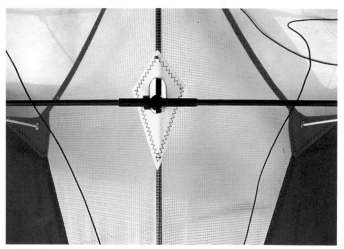

Add reinforcements carefully wherever rods are used to support the frame.

With the coming of stunt kites, workmanship continued to improve. Sail profiles are still constantly changing, making kites faster and more accurate. Various sail stretchers, shown in the photo to the left, preserve the original shape of the sail:

1. A notched shaft, with the aid of a rubber band or elastic bungi cord, stretches the side-bar pocket.
2. An end cap with a hole or an additional stretching device accommodates a rope at the towing edge.
3. A Velcro strip keeps the side-bar pocket either tight or loose.

Particularly important is how the sail is constructed at the points of highest stress. This is not only true for stunt kites.

A sail tends to tear most often where several parts of the frame structure come together. The photo on page 10 (above right) shows a device for holding stand-offs in place at the trailing edge. The trailing edge and sail were reinforced with heavy sailcloth, preventing premature wearing of the material. The photo on page 10 (below right) shows a similar construction. The reinforcements that have been added help prevent tearing, thereby extending the life of the kite.

Sewing Techniques

Interesting designs have a magical power. As soon as the flier of an intricately designed kite takes a break, people gather to admire the work of art. This closer look allows people to get an idea of how kites with such different designs are constructed. It may seem particularly hard to sew round or irregular shapes to the surface of the sail. Once you understand the special application and sewing techniques, it is easy to create even unusual shapes. The cat kites pictured below are examples of just such seemingly complicated designs.

If you can, start with a very basic kite and fly it before you add any designs to the sail. This is easy to do with a flat or a V-shaped kite; but it is not possible with a parafoil or box kite. Depending on the quality of workmanship involved, several different methods can be employed. In general, all use the zigzag stitch. This stitch tolerates tension well and has the advantage of adding a certain elasticity to the seam.

Sailcloth wrinkles and slips easily. If the sailcloth is wrinkled, iron it (at the "nylon" setting) before you start cutting. Also, remember that when the appliqués on the sail are in the vicinity of a seam, darker material should be placed over

lighter material. If done in reverse, the darker material will shine through the lighter where they overlap. Too, when correctly done the contrasts will be much more prominent.

When joining pieces, proceed as follows: first, sew small pieces together, then sew those finished pieces to larger ones. This eliminates undue stress on the material.

When applying designs to the sail, they must be pinned into place first. Even so, sometimes a piece will slip and the material underneath will wrinkle. A better method is to use cellophane tape instead of pins. You can sew right over the tape and remove it after you finish.

Appliqués made from nylon sailcloth can also be held in place with a fast-acting glue. Small dots of glue placed 1½ inches (4 cm) apart, on the underside, will hold the material in position; but you will have to work fast. A smooth working surface and wrinkle-free material are absolutely necessary. Another disadvantage of this method is that, particularly on light colors, the glue might leave dark shadows. You could try dissolving the glue, after the design has been sewn on, to make the spot disappear. Whatever you do, make sure that the appliqué is sewn on carefully and well because, over time, glue often disintegrates.

Sailcloth to which a layer of silicon has been added is particularly difficult to glue. If this is the material you are using, use a narrow, double-sided, cellophane tape, available in kite stores. Attach one side of the tape carefully along the edges of the appliqué. As with double-sided rug tape, the protective film is then removed and the appliqué is glued to the sail's surface. The disadvantage with this method is that, after a few stitches, glue begins to accumulate on the sewing needle and has to be constantly removed. The tape, however, remains in place and the design material can't slide out of position. This tape holds very securely so that even

An eye-catching appliqué design for a kite.

An extraordinary parafoil kite from Ed Wright of California.

larger designs can be easily applied using the zigzag stitch.

Some kite builders love to use the hot-tack method, where the pieces to be attached to the surface are "welded" to it with a fine-tip hot gun. This is the same tool used to burn designs into wood, and is available in hobby shops. The soldering or hot gun should be 20–25 watt, and the tip must be rounded and at a 30-degree angle. In addition, the tip should be slightly bent at the end. Use a metal file to sharpen the tip to the desired point. After the nylon pieces have been cut out and ironed, place them on a flat surface, overlapping them where they are to be joined. When the hot gun has reached the proper temperature, touch the material every 2 inches (5 cm) or so with the tip of the gun. The soldering points should be about ⅛ inch (0.2–0.3 cm) from the edge, and must have cooled off before you start sewing. Sew carefully. Try not to fold the material too much, often difficult when working with large pieces, or the weld might come lose. A sewing machine surface that is set level with the surface of the table you are working on, with about 8 to 12 inches (20–30 cm) of space to the left and the right of the sewing machine, is a great advantage. This allows you to spread the material out somewhat rather than fold it. Don't be concerned about the perforations created by the sewing needle; they do not weaken the seam. Even parafoils are sewn using this method. Although the holes are somewhat larger than those made by a sewing needle, the edges remain very strong due to the soldering.

After all the pieces have been sewn together, cut away the material—either from the back or the front—wherever you have a double layer. Use a small and very sharp, but not pointed, pair of scissors, and trim away the excess, leaving only about 1/16 inch (0.1 cm) outside of the zigzag seam. If dark material is covering a light cloth, the lighter material does not have to be removed. Leaving it, however, will add to

The Collado brothers are known for elaborate appliqué creations.

Some kite builders surprise spectators with perfect patchwork designs.

Fritz Jansmar has created this spectacular effect making very good use of the fine art of appliqué.

Kite artist George Peters impresses with his eye-catching and humorous kite shapes.

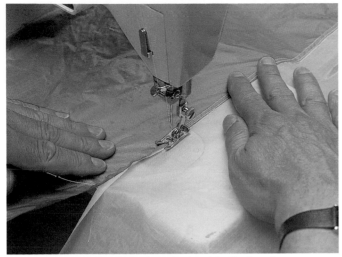

Set your sewing machine for 1-inch-wide (2–3 cm) seams when sewing sailcloth.

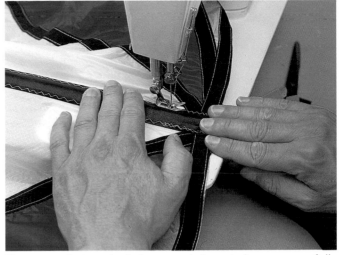

Sleeves, pockets and reinforcements have to be sewn carefully so that they can withstand additional stress.

Use a heavier needle for sewing waistbands and other reinforcements.

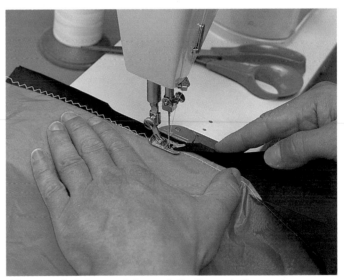

Always pull the material, carefully, through the sewing machine foot.

the overall weight and could influence the aerodynamics of the kite.

Sewing steps and helpful kite-making techniques are illustrated above:

Step 1: It is important to: (a) choose the proper stitch length (about ⅛ inch, 2–3 mm) for a French seam, and (b) the proper width (about ¼ inch, 5 mm) to sew the second seam parallel to the first. It is not necessary to pin the seam before sewing, but the seam must be placed flat (and parallel) on top of the material underneath. To avoid wrinkles, pull the material through gently.

Step 2: When sewing on pockets and sleeves, it might be necessary to change to a thicker needle or to adjust the tension of the upper and lower thread: a #7 sewing needle for nylon, a #9 needle for sewing the reinforcements on the sail. A tip for proper tension adjustment: loops on the top of the seam mean the lower tension is too loose or the upper tension too tight; loops on the underside of the seam mean the upper thread is too loose or the lower thread is too tight.

Steps 3 and 4: Sleeves for the side and vertical bars must always be reinforced, but this sewing can be done in several ways. These photos show two different techniques that have worked well: under stress, zigzag stitches give, while straight seams do less well under the same circumstances.

Generally speaking, sailcloth for stunt kites can be sewn with a #9 thread.

The kites shown on page 12, creations of Fritz Jansmar and George Peters, were made using the appliqué method and by sewing together pieces of cloth. While the latter method is much less complicated, only straight edges can be so joined. Two pieces are sewn together with the two-step French seam method shown on page 20. An open French seam is very strong and it is sewn with a straight stitch on the back of the sail. To avoid fraying of the nylon cloth, heat-seal the material along the edges or fold the French seam under before sewing it to the cloth.

Flying Lines for Stunt Kites

The kind of line used to maneuver your kite in the air is of utmost importance. Choose carefully; the wrong line can cause many problems. Pay special attention to the makeup and the weight of the line, as these directly influence a kite's flying ability.

Makeup: Some lines are twisted and others are made using a weaving process. The former consists of several individual strands that are twisted *around* each other. Woven lines consist of up to sixteen strands that are woven *into* each other. Both types are available in kite stores; woven lines are considered superior because they can be spliced.

Weight: In general, thin lines with high-tensile strength are better than thicker ones. The thinner line creates less wind resistance so allows the kite to reach a higher speed.

Line Material

Nylon lines have only limited use as flying line. Even though it is relatively impervious to humidity, nylon has a lower melting point and a rather rough surface. This is a disad-vantage because, to fly a stunt kite efficiently, the surface of the flying line should be as smooth as possible. When tying nylon line to a kite, be absolutely sure to use the bowline knot discussed on page 16. Seal the ends of the nylon line with the flame from a cigarette lighter.

Dacron lines consist of finely spun polyester fibre. Because of the tight weave, these lines are stronger than nylon lines. In addition, they have a smoother surface. However, Dacron lines are generally more expensive than nylon lines.

Kevlar lines are made from Aramid fibre. This material has an enormous resistance to tearing. Given the same strength, these lines are thinner than those made from polyester for a saving in weight and lower wind resistance. Another advantage is their relative resistance to stretching. This means that all steering movements are immediately transferred to the kite. Kevlar lines are also covered with a silicon layer which improves glide. The small diameter and the relative low friction-coefficient makes Kevlar line a high-tech material that allows perfect steering of a stunt kite.

Be careful with it, however: Kevlar has a high melting point and can easily cut other types of flying lines you may use in addition to Kevlar line. We also suggest that you wear gloves, when flying a kite with a Kevlar line, to avoid injuring your hands. Also, take care that Kevlar line does not get wet or come in contact with wet articles.

Spectra lines are made out of polyethylene and are even less subject to stretching than Kevlar lines. Because of their very smooth surface, they are well suited to flying stunt kites (see also page 77). One disadvantage of Spectra lines is that their melting point is lower than that of Kevlar; too, when coming in contact with other kite lines, they tear easily.

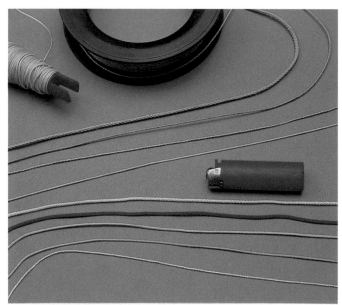

Kevlar or Dacron lines attached to horizontal steering bars makes perfect steering possible.

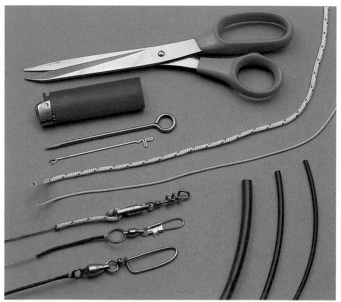

A variety of accessories and aids can help stunt kite builders attach lines to their creations.

Splicing Kevlar Lines

Lines that are knotted together reduces the tensile strength (average breaking load) in the knot by fifty percent. Since woven Kevlar lines are hollow inside, however, they can be inserted into each other instead of joined by knotting. When pulling the cord, the cover closes tightly around the ends, making a tight and secure connection. Steve Edeiken developed this "no-knot system" for splicing kite lines (see step-by-step instructional diagrams 1a–7a):

1a: Push the line together to loosen the mesh.

2a: About 2 inches (5 cm) from the end of the line, insert an open latch hook into the hollow cord. Exit about 2½ inches (6 cm) farther down, then grab and pull the cord at that point through the inside.

3a: The loop is pulled through to the right.

4a: Holding on to the loop with the right hand, push on the double layer of line, rolling that end towards the left (inside out).

5a: The end of the cord is now on the left.

6a: The open latch hook is again inserted about 2½ inches (6 cm) below where the cord end is sticking out. Catch the end and pull it inside the cord.

7a: Finished loop.

Loop Protection

To avoid damage to the line, a protective covering can be placed over it: diagrams 1b–3b. A "shrinking" sleeve is placed over the splice, and the loop is pulled over the sleeve. The new loop you have created accommodates the carabineer (spring-loaded clamp). Shrink the sleeve over a heat source (don't worry, Kevlar has a high melting point).

A Spectra line can't be spliced because the hollow space inside is too small. Instead, slip a protective covering over the line and, as shown in diagrams 1c–5c, tie it into a loop. The protective sleeve reduces friction in the knot and the possibility of breakage. Kite stores have splicing kits available that contain everything you need.

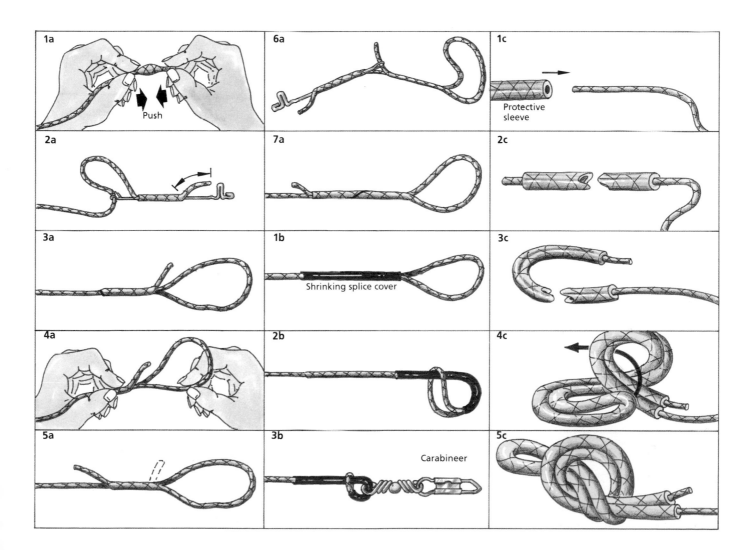

1a — Push

2a

3a

4a

5a

6a

7a

1b — Shrinking splice cover

2b

3b — Carabineer

1c — Protective sleeve

2c

3c

4c

5c

Knots

Choosing the right knots and making the knot properly can influence the flying ability and safety of your stunt kite enormously. When done correctly, these knots are very sturdy but can easily be untied when necessary. Practise first with a thick rope. Knowing how to tie a bowline knot, a weaver's knot, and a round turn half hitch is indispensable when it comes to attaching bridle and flying lines. Lines with the same diameter are tied together with a fisherman's knot. (Keep in mind, however, that the tensile strength in a knot is reduced by fifty percent.) The figure-eight knot is used to prevent the end of a line from slipping out of the knot.

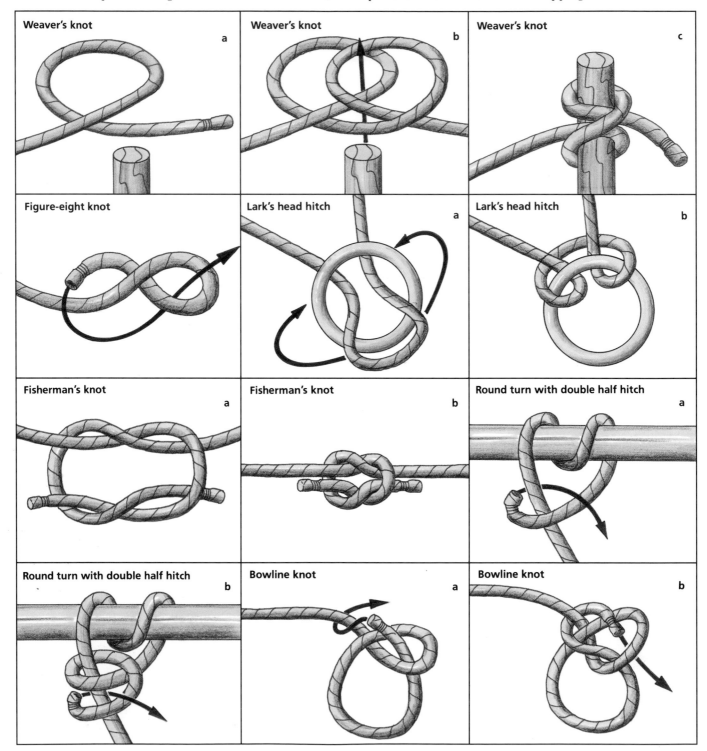

Weaver's knot · a
Weaver's knot · b
Weaver's knot · c
Figure-eight knot
Lark's head hitch · a
Lark's head hitch · b
Fisherman's knot · a
Fisherman's knot · b
Round turn with double half hitch · a
Round turn with double half hitch · b
Bowline knot · a
Bowline knot · b

Reels and Accessories

For good kite control, your choice of reel is very important. Round reels (1) are popular and excellent for flying because the length of flying line can be easily adjusted or varied. The reel itself provides the flier with a good grip, but it is necessary to hold the reel tightly, so that the line does not reel off continuously. The H reel (2) is equipped with a hook that allows you to fix the line in place at any time; this is easier on your hands.

Using a reel has its disadvantages: you can't always get optimal use of the flying line, and the hook might break off. Loops (3) are a good alternative. A loop slips over your hand and stays in place over the ball of the thumb. Loops allow good transfer of your movements from the hand to the flying line and, therefore, to the kite. Lines, however, must be wound onto a reel (for instance, an H reel) separately. Also, the length of the flying line cannot be adjusted as it must be completely reeled out in order to be fastened to the respective loop.

The baton reel (4) is another possibility; the end of the steering line is fastened to the handle. This reel gives you a good grip, but it is hard to rewind the line.

Another accessory, important in stunt kite flying, is the tube-shaped tail (6). From 4 to 10 inches (10–25 cm) long, these tails made of foil are affixed to the kite. When the kite is airborne, the maneuvers "paint beautiful pictures" in the sky. Reinforce the tails at both ends with duct tape to prevent fraying. Use fluorescent rods (7), when flying your kite at night, so that the figures the kite performs will be visible.

Steering Rods/Bars

When your stunt kite or a train creates a lot of pull, it makes sense to use a steering rod. This device provides a good grip and favorably transfers your steering movements to the kite.

Most steering rods also serve as reels. If that is not the case, the flying line must be wound onto a separate H-reel (photo below left). Generally speaking, the length of flying line cannot be varied when using a steering rod, since the line must be totally unwound. This problem, however, is not a difficult one to solve: gather and tie together any excess line, as shown in the photos on page 76. Attach two strong rings to the steering lines, as shown in the knots diagrams on page 16, and connect the ends with a snap-link.

The photo below right shows steering rods made of wood (1) and (2); (1) with the steering line wound up, (2) showing the notched ends. Another steering rod (3) is made of aluminum; hooks or clamps allow the line to be reeled off or on. A steering-reel rod (4), hand constructed from aluminum or NIRO tubes, has a particularly good load-carrying capacity and can also accommodate a trapeze or a safety belt (5). Trapeze pants, used in sailing, are excellent for use with a steering rod. Steering rods are available in kite stores; trapeze pants and safety belts are usually available in stores that carry sailing equipment.

A steering rod for a small kite can be built easily and with very little expense. The steering lines can be wound around the steering rod either during or after the flight. On wooden rods, the lines wind from end notch to end notch; on aluminum or NIRO rods, around the attached anvils.

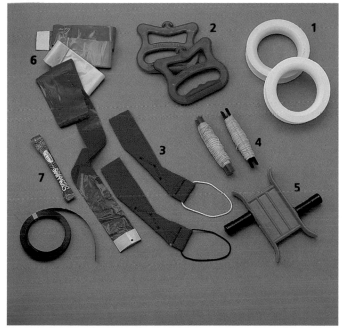

The choice of reels is an important factor for good kite control and a perfect kite-flying experience.

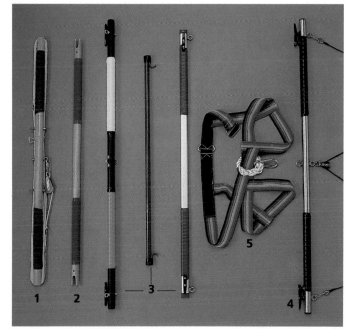

Steering rods equipped with a trapeze are very helpful for kites that have exceptionally strong pulling power.

Tools

Most of the tools you will need to build a kite are probably already in your toolbox. The most important are scissors to cut the nylon sailcloth. Be sure that your scissors are sharp; it is difficult to make straight, true cuts if they are dull. In fact, it is best to put one pair of scissors aside and use it only for cutting nylon, investing in a second pair for cutting all other materials. If necessary, as when making single-fold hems, nylon can also be hot-cut with a special tool or soldering gun.

The following tools are needed to mark patterns and identify specific places on rods or struts for cut-outs or special attachments: a ruler, an angle iron, and—for the precision-conscious—a caliper rule. You also need a hobby saw to cut the rods for the frame. The cut edges also need to be carefully smoothed out with a file—take special care when working on fibreglass or graphite rods (consider using a mask). The ends of the rods must be covered with plastic end caps.

Connecting tubes are cut to size with a knife; a carpenter's knife with an adjustable blade works best. You can cut notches into tube sections with a very sharp knife as well.

If instructions call for grommets and hollow rivets (on sails or tube sections), a grommet tool and a hole-puncher are indispensable. These tools are available in hobby and craft stores. Even if well-functioning tools do not guarantee that your kite will take off and fly perfectly, they are, nevertheless, important to success.

Sewing Accessories

Maneuverable kites are exposed to more than normal stress. A crash, sail flutter, and the influence of powerful pull winds are so great that the materials used age rather quickly. For that reason, it is very important that, when reinforcements are attached on corners, sleeves, pockets, and connecting points, the recommended sewing techniques are followed very carefully. The accessories needed, shown in the photo below left, are available in kite stores.

Dacron remnants (1): small leftover pieces of Dacron are used to reinforce those corners and edges that are exposed to particular stress, such as sleeves and tube connectors. Small pockets can also be made from Dacron remnants; Dacron will stretch when exposed to excessive stress.

Dacron binding (2): Dacron is also available in strips (in various colors and widths). These strips are sewn into the seam as reinforcement. If Dacron is not available in a specific width, you can make it yourself from a larger piece, using the hot-cutting method.

Waistbands (3): Wherever a sail is exposed to excessive stress, like the head of the sail, you must use a piece of waistband for reinforcement. This elastic material can withstand a great deal of stress but it is also heavier than Dacron.

Self-adhesive nylon (4): This material is extremely practical. It is used on places of minimal stress and is easy to work with because the material won't slip when being sewn.

Velcro (5): Velcro is used for pockets and sleeves. Also, a carrying bag is easy to open and close if you use Velcro.

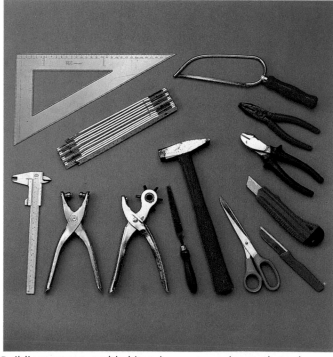

Building maneuverable kites does not require costly tools. Simple hole-puncher and grommet tools are easily available.

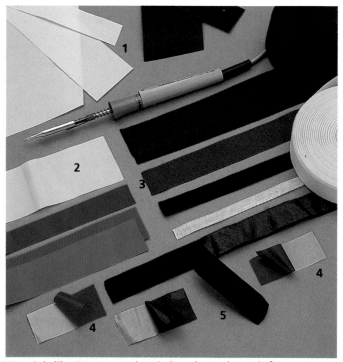

Materials like Dacron and waistbands used to reinforce stress points should be prepared using the hot-cutting method.

Tuning a Stunt Kite

The trailing edges of stunt kites often tend to flutter, creating considerable noise. As the photo below shows, it is the outer edges that are most affected. Fluttering also acts as a brake, slowing the speed of the kite. Precision fliers make use of this effect; steering the kite into a curve, speed slows drastically, allowing for more precision. Kite builders who are bothered by the resulting noise, however, have found several ways to deal with it:

1. Use a particularly stiff nylon sailcloth. Experts use cloth made of polyester or Dacron.
2. Give the back trailing edge a concave curve. Wind pressure passing underneath will cause the sail to tighten, eliminating the flutter.
3. Sew a nylon cord into the seam and use it to tighten the trailing edge (see photo below left and on page 34).
4. Use bias tape or Dacron to reinforce the trailing edges (see page 46).

5. When cutting the pattern, give the sail a "little belly." Under wind pressure, the tension in that area will increase, reducing flutter.
6. Add gauze parallel to the trailing edge (photo right, above). This reduces the pressure on the edge and, thereby, the noise.
7. Sew small pockets on the sail. Wind caught in these pockets gives shape to the sail and, again, reduces fluttering.

The ideal sail is one that accommodates the effect the kite is to have and, more often then not, a kite builder will use a combination of the above-mentioned techniques.

Stand-offs added to the trailing edge also counteract fluttering. Too, under extreme conditions, the thin rods improve the kite's flight capability: in a high wind, the kite is easier to maneuver and the possibility of a crash is reduced. The photo (right, below) shows several ways of attaching stand-offs to a sail.

Different methods of treating trailing edges.

High pressure on the trailing edge of a kite produces fluttering which results in annoying noises.

Adding stand-offs clearly improves the aerodynamic performance of a kite in flight.

Building a Kite

Following are full instructions for crafting kites which I have not only built but flown successfully. The kite-building designs provide a wide variety of techniques in case some of the materials needed are not readily available. The letters in parentheses refer you to the relevant drawing; the numbers provide measurements also in metric. (See the comparative measurements chart here for precise fractional-inch breakdown. See here also drawings of specialized techniques used in constructing various of the following kites.)

Do read all of the instructions carefully from beginning to end before buying materials and tools and always test out interlocking parts or connectors at point of purchase for proper fit. And, when you are finally ready for that first flight, find a wide-open space: in order to tune your new kite properly, you will need even wind conditions. Tips for flying and tuning your kite are provided in later chapters.

Comparative Measurements

INCHES			(CM)	INCHES			(CM)
	1/64	0.01563	(0.03969)		33/64	0.51563	(1.30969)
1/32		0.03125	(0.07938)	17/32		0.53125	(1.34938)
	3/64	0.04688	(0.11906)		35/64	0.54688	(1.38906)
1/16		0.06250	(0.15875)	9/16		0.56250	(1.42875)
	5/64	0.07813	(0.19844)		37/64	0.57813	(1.46844)
3/32		0.09375	(0.23813)	19/32		0.59375	(1.50813)
	7/64	0.10938	(0.27781)		39/64	0.60938	(1.54781)
1/8		0.12500	(0.31750)	5/8		0.62500	(1.58750)
	9/64	0.14063	(0.35719)		41/64	0.64063	(1.62719)
5/32		0.15625	(0.39688)	21/32		0.65625	(1.66688)
	11/64	0.17188	(0.43656)		43/64	0.67188	(1.70656)
3/16		0.18750	(0.47625)	11/16		0.68750	(1.74625)
	13/64	0.20313	(0.51594)		45/64	0.70313	(1.78594)
7/32		0.21875	(0.55563)	23/32		0.71875	(1.82563)
	15/64	0.23438	(0.59531)		47/64	0.73438	(1.86531)
1/4		0.25000	(0.63500)	3/4		0.75000	(1.90500)
	17/64	0.26563	(0.67469)		49/64	0.76563	(1.94469)
9/32		0.28125	(0.71438)	25/32		0.78125	(1.98438)
	19/64	0.29688	(0.75406)		51/64	0.79688	(2.02406)
5/16		0.31250	(0.79375)	13/16		0.81250	(2.06375)
	21/64	0.32813	(0.83344)		53/64	0.82813	(2.10344)
11/32		0.34375	(0.87313)	27/32		0.84375	(2.14313)
	23/64	0.35938	(0.91281)		55/64	0.85938	(2.18281)
3/8		0.37500	(0.95250)	7/8		0.87500	(2.22250)
	25/64	0.39063	(0.99219)		57/64	0.89063	(2.26219)
13/32		0.40625	(1.03188)	29/32		0.90625	(2.30188)
	27/64	0.42188	(1.07156)		59/64	0.92188	(2.34156)
7/16		0.43750	(1.11125)	11/16		0.93750	(2.38125)
	29/64	0.45313	(1.15094)		61/64	0.95313	(2.42094)
15/32		0.46875	(1.19063)	31/32		0.96875	(2.46063)
	31/64	0.48438	(1.23031)		63/64	0.98438	(2.50031)
1/2		0.50000	(1.27000)	1		1.00000	(2.54000)

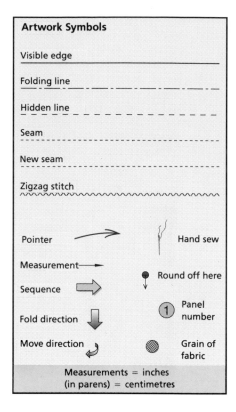

Artwork Symbols

Visible edge

Folding line

Hidden line

Seam

New seam

Zigzag stitch

Pointer

Measurement

Sequence

Fold direction

Move direction

Hand sew

Round off here

Panel number

Grain of fabric

Measurements = inches
(in parens) = centimetres

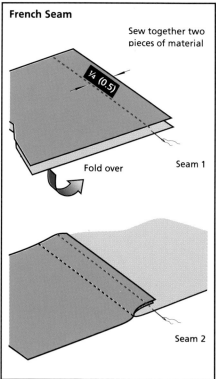

French Seam

Sew together two pieces of material

¼ (0.5)

Fold over

Seam 1

Seam 2

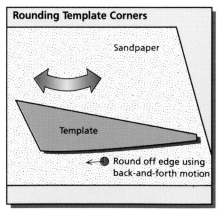

Rounding Template Corners

Sandpaper

Template

Round off edge using back-and-forth motion

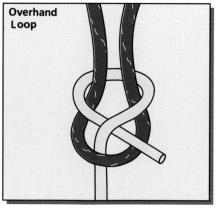

Overhand Loop

Stunt Kites

SOLAR FIRE

If you like fast kites, Solar Fire is a good choice. Graphite rods and flat sail surfaces give this kite enormous speed. The bowed sails, due to the slightly curved seam, also add considerable tension along the trailing edge, resulting in almost silent flight. Short standoffs make it possible to fly the kite high against the wind, without the wind being forced away from the sail and causing a crash.

The Solar Fire can be flown in winds of from 2.5 to 6 (light to strong breeze) according to the Beaufort scale and is also well suited to flying in high-speed wind conditions. Forces created during such high speeds usually remain within the kite's tolerable limits. Beginners, however, are advised to start at lower wind speeds (around 3) so that they can get used to the kite's enormous flying

capabilities. Use a flight line that can withstand a force of 168 to 210 pounds (80–100 kg) of pressure.

Tuning must proceed in small steps, making adjustments one millimetre at a time. First, establish a good balance, as indicated in the diagram. Because seam widths may vary, balance may also vary from one kite to the next. Attack angles are easily changed by adjusting the position of the balancing rings.

Go first to a kite specialty store when you are shopping for building material, but remember that hobby shops often carry kite-related items.

Note: Protect your eyes and hands, and do not inhale the dust and/or vapors when working with graphite and fibreglass-reinforced materials or while hot-cutting sailcloth. Synthetic materials can be hazardous.

Building Material

2¼ sq yd (1.8 m²) various color nylon sailcloth, 1⅜ oz/sq yd (45 g/m²)

2¼ sq yd (1.8 m²) cardboard or plywood

7 graphite rods, 32½ in (82.5 cm) long, 0.234 in (0.59 cm) ⌀

2 aluminum connectors, 2 in (5 cm) long, 0.234 in (0.59 cm) inside ⌀

1 fibreglass rod, 13¾ in (35 cm) long, 0.118 in (0.3 cm) ⌀

4 vinyl end caps, ⅛ in (0.3 cm) inside ⌀, ⁵⁄₁₆ in (0.8 cm) outside ⌀

1 PVC hose, 8 in (20 cm) long, 0.237 in (0.6 cm) inside ⌀

1 high-pressure hose, 1³⁄₁₆ in (3 cm) long, ¼ in (0.6 cm) inside ⌀

1 Dacron bias tape, 103 in (260 cm) long, 2 in (5 cm) wide

1 Dacron bias tape, 29½ in (75 cm) long, 1 in (2.5 cm) wide

3 arrow nocks, ¼ in (0.59 cm) inside ⌀

Diagram

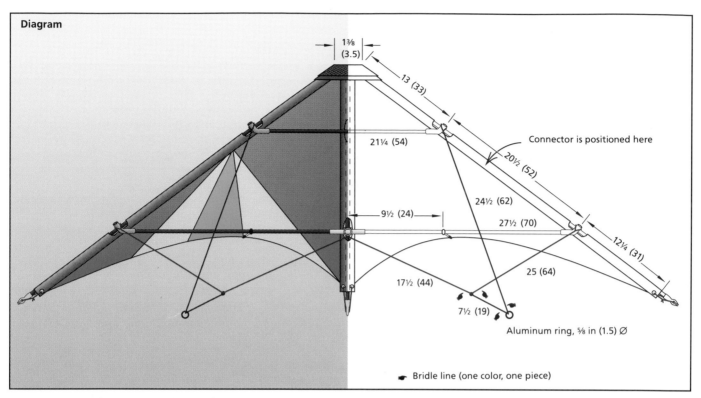

1⅜ (3.5)

13 (33)

Connector is positioned here

21¼ (54)

20½ (52)

9½ (24)

24½ (62)

27½ (70)

12¼ (31)

17½ (44)

25 (64)

7½ (19)

Aluminum ring, ⅝ in (1.5) Ø

⬅ Bridle line (one color, one piece)

1 elastic cord, 11¾ in (30 cm) long, ⅛ in (0.3 cm) wide

1 aluminum connector, 2⅜ in (6 cm) long, 0.234 in (0.59 cm) Ø

1 waistband, 4¾ in (12 cm) long, 1½ in (4 cm) wide

4 grommets, ³⁄₁₆ in (0.5 cm) Ø

1 Dacron line, 5½ yd (500 cm) long, ¹⁄₃₂ in (0.1 cm) Ø

2 cable connectors, ⅛ in (0.3 cm) wide fibreglass-reinforced tape

1 elastic cord, 11¾ in (30 cm) long, ⅛ in (0.3 cm) wide

2 key rings, ⅝ in (1.5 cm) Ø

Building Instructions

First, make templates for the five sail sections. With templates on hand, you will be able to reproduce this kite whenever you want. If you plan to build this model several times, use thin plywood for the templates. (See measurements in diagram A.) If using cardboard, cut out the template using a sharp carpet knife. To shape the sail, place a sheet of rough sandpaper on a flat surface and use it to round off the corners, creating an even curve. Start about 8 inches (20 cm) above each end. The corner itself is shortened by about ³⁄₁₆ of an inch (0.4 cm). (See also drawing on page 20.)

A Sail Pattern

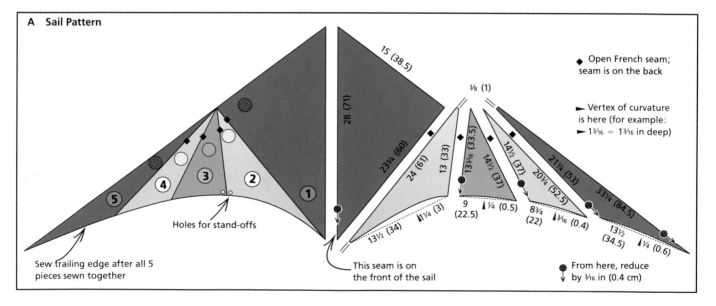

15 (38.5)

♦ Open French seam; seam is on the back

⬆ Vertex of curvature is here (for example: 1³⁄₁₆ = 1³⁄₁₆ in deep)

28 (71)

⅜ (1)

23¾ (60)

24 (61)

13 (33)

13³⁄₁₆ (33.5)

14½ (37)

14½ (37)

20¾ (52.5)

21¼ (53)

33¼ (84.5)

9 (22.5)

¼ (0.5)

8¾ (22)

³⁄₁₆ (0.4)

13½ (34.5)

¼ (0.6)

13½ (34)

¼ (3)

⬤ From here, reduce by ³⁄₁₆ in (0.4 cm)

Holes for stand-offs

Sew trailing edge after all 5 pieces sewn together

This seam is on the front of the sail

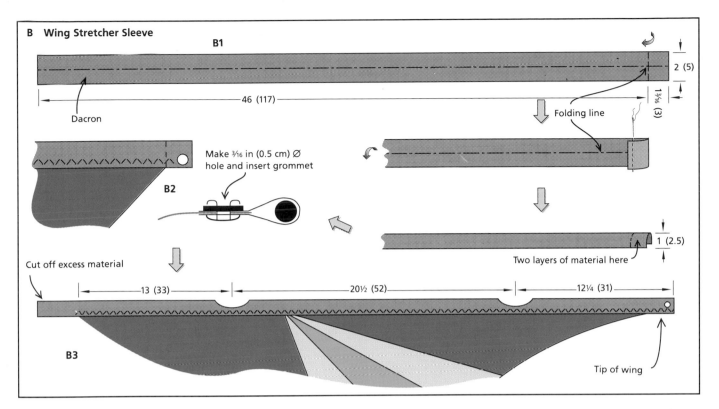

B Wing Stretcher Sleeve

B1

2 (5)

46 (117)

1³⁄₁₆ (3)

Dacron

Folding line

Make ³⁄₁₆ in (0.5 cm) Ø hole and insert grommet

B2

1 (2.5)

Two layers of material here

Cut off excess material

13 (33) 20½ (52) 12¼ (31)

B3

Tip of wing

Only the points marked with the red dot symbol are rounded off.

Next, cut out all ten parts of the sail with a hot knife. Pay special attention to the direction of the grain (A). Don't use too many different colors for your kite; you will already be attracting a lot of attention by performing spectacular flight stunts. The different sections are sewn together as follows: first, join to-gether one half and then the other half. The seams are on the back. With both halves sewn together, lay them next to each other. At this point, if the trailing edges are uneven, use the hot knife to even them off. Use the curve of the template as your guide. Now, make a double-folded hem on the trailing edge of each half (see page 22). The seam of the double hem is on the back of the sail and should be about ¼ inch (0.6 cm) wide. The seams of the double hem should be slightly less, about ³⁄₁₆ inch (0.4 cm) apart. When sewing both halves together, make sure that the seam is on the front of the sail.

Now, prepare the side-bar sleeve, made from a 48-inch-long (120 cm) Dacron strip. Fold the strip as shown in the diagram (B1). The cut-outs for the

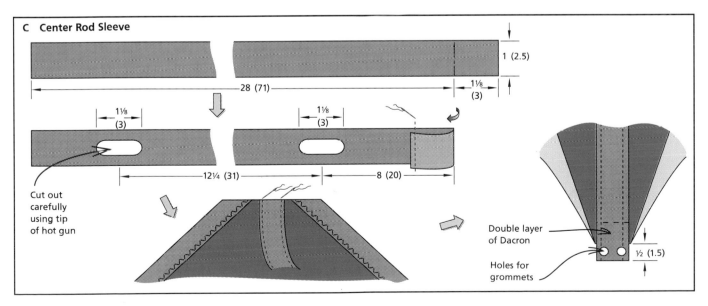

C Center Rod Sleeve

1 (2.5)

28 (71) 1⅛ (3)

1⅛ (3) 1⅛ (3)

Cut out carefully using tip of hot gun

12¼ (31) 8 (20)

Double layer of Dacron

Holes for grommets

½ (1.5)

side-bar connectors are made with the hot knife (B3).

Start sewing at the tip of the wing with the zigzag stitch. Push the nylon into the Dacron sleeve about ⅜ inch (1 cm). As illustrated in the drawing, the Dacron material is doubled on the tip of the wing; this will later accommodate the grommets. The center bar sleeve is sewn on top of the seam on the front of the sail. The cut-outs are, again, made with a hot-cutter or soldering gun. Do not make sharp edges, as they are prone to tear later on. The Dacron, with two simple seams, is sewn directly over the middle seams, covering up the stitching.

The tip of the kite is reinforced so that, in case of a crash, the graphite rods will not tear through the material. First, place a layer of Dacron about 2 inches (5 cm) wide over the tip and sew it following diagram D. Then, fold the bias tape, 9¾ inches (12 cm) long and 1½ inches (4 cm) wide, over the tip and, using a thicker needle, sew the Dacron and bias tape together.

First, make the left and then the right seam of the center bar sleeve; then hem the outside. Now, remove excess material with a hot knife.

The kite sail is now completed. Next, attach each of the four ³⁄₁₆-inch (0.5 cm) ∅ grommets, to the tips of the sails and at the ends of the center bar sleeve. With the tip of a hot gun make a 1½-inch-wide (4 cm) hole in the Dacron (B).

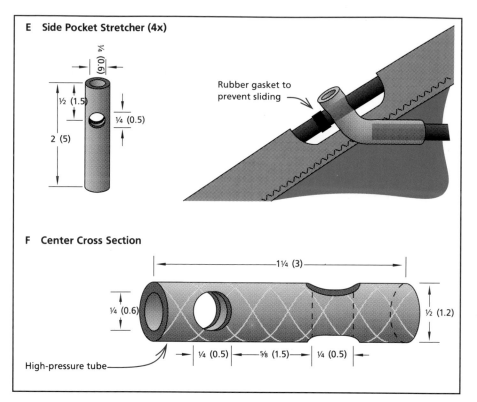

E Side Pocket Stretcher (4x)

Rubber gasket to prevent sliding

¼ (0.6)
½ (1.5)
2 (5)
¼ (0.5)

F Center Cross Section

1¼ (3)
¼ (0.6)
½ (1.2)
High-pressure tube
¼ (0.5) ⅝ (1.5) ¼ (0.5)

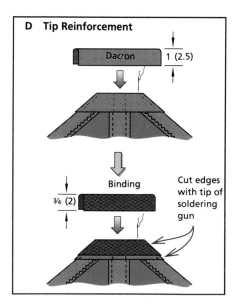

D Tip Reinforcement

Dacron
1 (2.5)

Binding
¾ (2)

Cut edges with tip of soldering gun

It does not matter if the soldering tip touches the seams, the edges of the grommets will protect them. Grommets are hollow rivets that can be bought at any hardware store or hobby shop. The grommets are fastened to the material with a special pair of pliers. Two grommets are fastened to each end of the center bar sleeve. They, together with the help of ⅛-inch (0.3 cm) ∅ rubber cord, are used to stretch the sails. A 1-inch-long (2.5 cm) loop is pulled through the hole of the grommet at the tip of the kite, with the end tied into a knot to keep the loop from sliding through the hole. First, tie the end of the rubber cord at the center bar sleeve into a simple knot. The elastic band is first pulled through one grommet and then through the other, and the ends are also tied into a knot. Make sure you have about 1³⁄₁₆ inches (3 cm) play in the cord.

Each side-bar sleeve gets two PVC tube connectors with 0.237 inch (0.6 cm) inside ∅. Cut four 2-inch-long (5 cm) pieces, punch a ³⁄₁₆-inch (0.5 cm) ∅ hole into each (E). Tools are available in hobby or kite stores.

The center crosspiece is made from high-pressure tubing, 0.237 inch (0.6 cm) inside ∅. These tubes have an additional layer of nylon fibre that is designed to increase their strength. They work well as connectors that are exposed to high stress. Two holes, each ³⁄₁₆ inch (0.5 cm) ∅, are punched opposite each other in the tubing. Pay special attention to the measurements given in drawing F.

Graphite rods 0.234 inch (0.59 cm) in ∅ are used for the frame. Side bars are made using one and a half rods each, so cut a 32½-inch-long (82.5 cm) rod in half. The halves are used for the left and the right side bars. Connect one whole and one half rod with an aluminum sleeve and glue into place. The sleeves are available in kite stores. Slide the side bars into their respective sleeves. The connector tubes are slipped over the rods at the cut-outs. If this is difficult, a touch of bar soap will make it easier.

The rods should be only about 1 inch (2.5 cm) longer than the sleeves; if they are much longer, shorten them accordingly. The sleeves are stretched with the help of arrow shafts and or bungi cord.

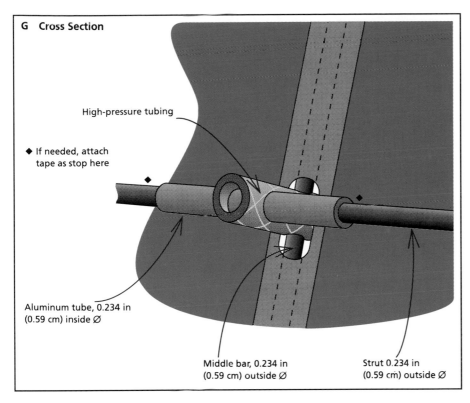

G Cross Section

High-pressure tubing

◆ If needed, attach tape as stop here

Aluminum tube, 0.234 in (0.59 cm) inside ∅

Middle bar, 0.234 in (0.59 cm) outside ∅

Strut 0.234 in (0.59 cm) outside ∅

the rods from sliding, use fibreglass-reinforced tape instead. The front strut is inserted in the center bar. Stand-offs prevent loss of wind power in extreme flight situations. Here is one way to attach the rods; of course, you can also use one of the other methods discussed on pages 37 and 49.

Using the fine tip of the hot gun, punch two holes to the left and right of the seam on the trailing edge (A). Make sure that the thread of the seam is not damaged. Attach a vinyl end cap with a ⅛-inch (0.3 cm) ∅ cable fastener (H). Fit two more end caps over the back strut. Fibreglass-reinforced stand-offs, about 5½ inches (14 cm) long and 0.118 inch (0.3 cm) ∅, are now inserted into the end caps (I). To make sure that they stay in place, the ends of the rods can be covered with fibreglass-reinforced tape.

Attach the bridle as shown in the diagram on page 22. Make sure that the key ring is equipped with an adjustable loop. The loop allows you to change the takeup angle according to the prevailing wind speed.

The center bar is made from one piece. The cross piece is placed at the cut-out in the back (see drawing). The rod of 0.234 inch (0.59 cm) ∅ is cut to size after it is inserted in its sleeve. It should extend the sleeve by 1 inch (2.5 cm). Arrow shafts and elastic cord are again used here for stretching.

The small front strut is 21½ inches (54 cm) long. Cut a rod to size and insert it in the tubes prepared for them (E). The aluminum connector for the back strut is placed in the high-pressure tubing of the cross section. Both back struts are 28 inches (70 cm) long. Cut the rods to size and insert them into the aluminum connector and the hose section of the side bar (G). If the aluminum connector is not fitted with a stop, which is needed to prevent

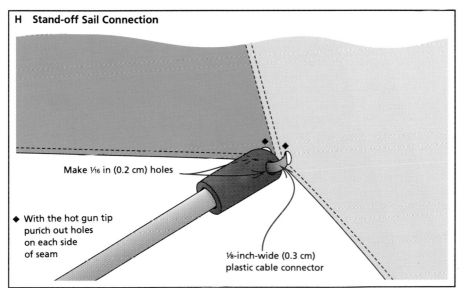

H Stand-off Sail Connection

Make 1/16 in (0.2 cm) holes

◆ With the hot gun tip punch out holes on each side of seam

⅛-inch-wide (0.3 cm) plastic cable connector

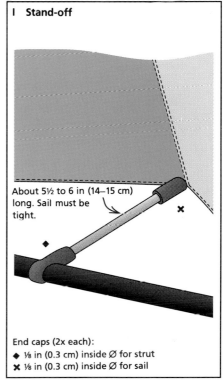

I Stand-off

About 5½ to 6 in (14–15 cm) long. Sail must be tight.

End caps (2x each):
◆ ⅛ in (0.3 cm) inside ∅ for strut
✕ ⅛ in (0.3 cm) inside ∅ for sail

BEL AIR

We distinguish between classes of maneuverable kites. Sail surface and weight play a large role in the classification. The Bel Air pictured above weighs only a little over 3½ ounces, or 100 grams, which makes it an excellent light-wind kite. This kite will demonstrate the advantages it has with as little as a number 2 (Beaufort) wind: precision flight, quick reaction to steering maneuvers, and a huge flight radius. The weight of the building material was vital in the selection. Of course, the kite can also be built for stronger winds, in which case one would choose stronger rods for the frame. Sewing the Bel Air is particularly hard, so it is not a good project for someone who has not had a lot of experience using a sewing machine.

The sails of the Bel Air are designed so that they already have a built-in profile, which gives the kite good climbing abilities. For the first test flight, and the balancing connected with it, it is important to have even wind conditions. "Even," in this connection, means without trees, houses, or hills nearby that could create wind turbulence. Turbulent, uneven winds will give wrong readings. Once the proper balance is established, with the help of markings, it is easy to adjust the climbing angle to the velocity of the wind on any given day. To fly this kite you need a line that will tolerate about 175 to 225 pounds (80–100 kg) of pull.

Note: To avoid health problems make sure that you do not inhale the dust created when cutting graphite or fibreglass-reinforced rods or the vapors when hot-cutting or working with a soldering gun; both are dangerous to your health.

Building Material

1¾ sq yd (1.3 m²) various color nylon sailcloth, 1 oz/sq yd (32 g/m²)

1⅝ sq yd (1.3 m²) cardboard or plywood

7 graphite rods, 32½ in (82.5 cm) long, 0.197 in (0.5 cm) ∅

1 fibreglass-reinforced rod, 160 in (400 cm) long, 0.079 in (0.2 cm) ∅

2 vinyl end caps, ¹⁄₁₆ in (0.2 cm) ∅

2 vinyl end caps, ³⁄₁₆ in (0.4 cm) ∅

1 hose, 80 in (200 cm) long, 0.197 in (0.5 cm) inside ∅

1 hose, 6 in (15 cm) long, ⅛ in (0.3 cm) inside ∅

Diagram

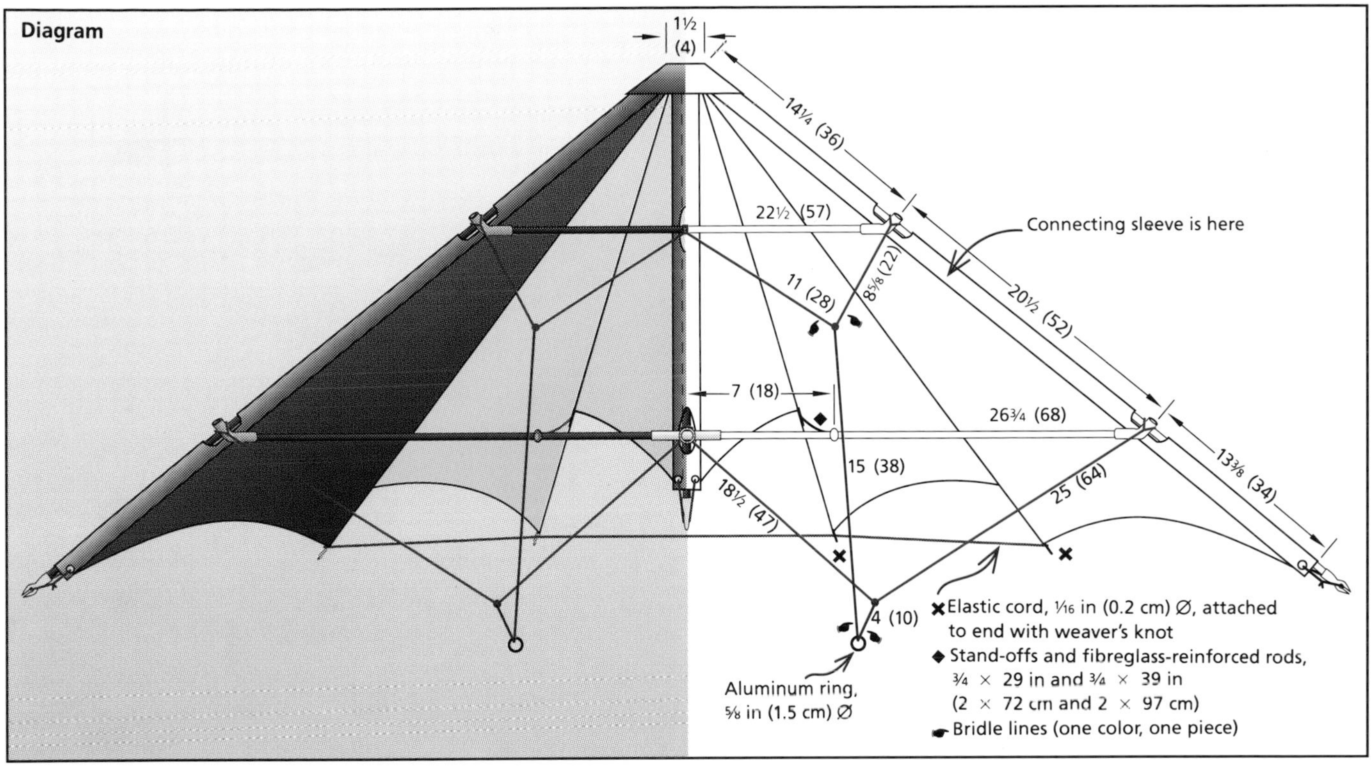
1½ (4)
14¼ (36)
22½ (57)
Connecting sleeve is here
11 (28)
8⅝ (22)
20½ (52)
7 (18)
26¾ (68)
15 (38)
18½ (47)
25 (64)
13⅜ (34)
4 (10)
Aluminum ring, ⅝ in (1.5 cm) Ø
✖ Elastic cord, 1/16 in (0.2 cm) Ø, attached to end with weaver's knot
◆ Stand-offs and fibreglass-reinforced rods, ¾ × 29 in and ¾ × 39 in (2 × 72 cm and 2 × 97 cm)
Bridle lines (one color, one piece)

1 hose, 1½ in (4 cm) long, 3/16 in (0.4 cm) inside Ø
1 hose, 1⅛ in (3 cm) long, ¼ in (0.6 cm) inside Ø
1 Dacron bias tape, 104 in (260 cm) long, 1½ in (4 cm) wide
1 Dacron bias tape, 30 in (75 cm) long, ¾ in (2 cm) wide
1 section of Dacron, 6 by 7 in (15 × 18 cm)
3 arrow nocks, 0.197 in (0.5 cm) inside Ø
2 aluminum connectors, 2⅜ in (6 cm) long, 0.197 in (0.5 cm) inside Ø
1 elastic cord, 68 in (170 cm) long, 1/16 in (0.2 cm) inside Ø
1 Dacron line, 1/32 in (0.1 cm) Ø
2 aluminum rings, ⅝ in (1.5 cm) Ø
1 Dacron line, 5½ yd (500 cm) long, 1/32 in (0.1 cm) Ø

Building Instructions

Make templates from cardboard or plywood according to the measurements shown in A. With sandpaper, carefully round off the corners of the template marked by the red-dot symbols in A; make sure that the curves are even and are reduced by 3/16 of an inch (0.4 cm). (See instruction on page 20).

A Sail Pattern

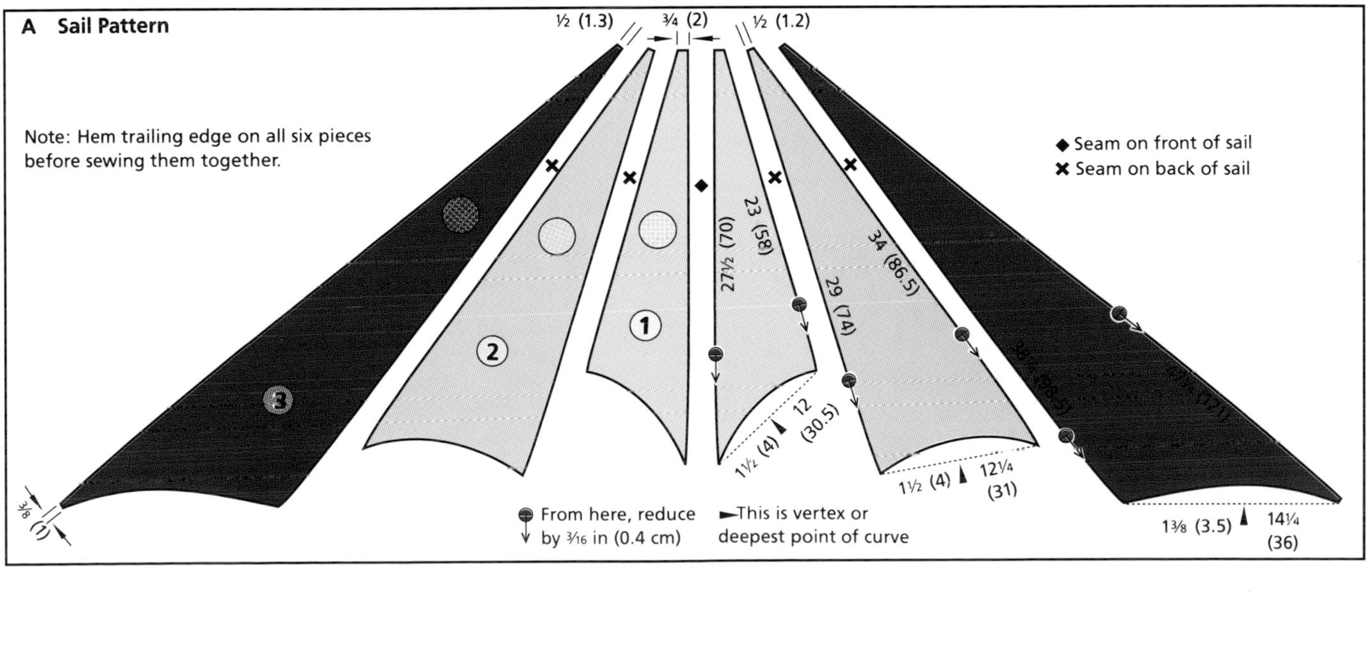
½ (1.3)
¾ (2)
½ (1.2)
Note: Hem trailing edge on all six pieces before sewing them together.
◆ Seam on front of sail
✖ Seam on back of sail
1
2
3
27½ (70)
23 (58)
29 (74)
34 (86.5)
12 (30.5)
1½ (4)
12¼ (31)
1½ (4)
1⅜ (3.5)
14¼ (36)
⅜ (1)
From here, reduce by 3/16 in (0.4 cm)
This is vertex or deepest point of curve

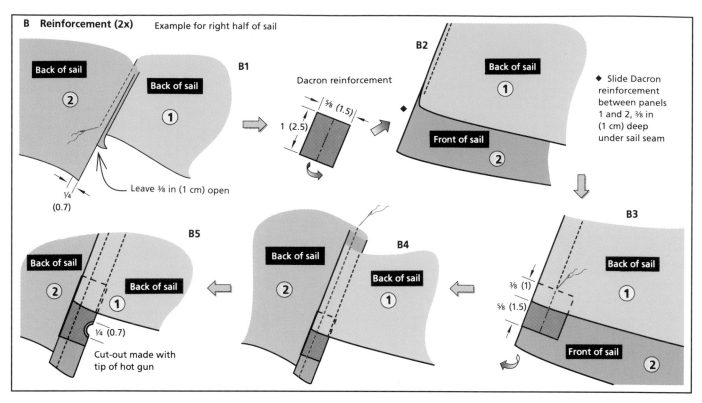

B Reinforcement (2x)   Example for right half of sail

B1

Back of sail ②   Back of sail ①

Leave ⅜ in (1 cm) open

¼ (0.7)

Dacron reinforcement

⅝ (1.5)

1 (2.5)

B2

Back of sail ①

Front of sail ②

◆ Slide Dacron reinforcement between panels 1 and 2, ⅜ in (1 cm) deep under sail seam

B3

Back of sail ①

⅜ (1)

⅝ (1.5)

Front of sail ②

B5

Back of sail ②   Back of sail ①

¼ (0.7)

Cut-out made with tip of hot gun

B4

Back of sail ②   Back of sail ①

Now, using the templates, cut out six sections for the sail. A hot knife makes the job easier and prevents later fraying of the edges of the nylon. Pay attention to the grain of the fabric.

Make a double-folded hem at the trailing edges in the back. Stand-offs are attached where sections 1 and 2 join. Reinforce the sail here with an extra piece of Dacron material. Sew

sections 1 and 2 together as shown in B1, making sure that ⅜ inch (1 cm) of the seam at the end of section 1 remains open. Slide a piece of Dacron cloth ⅝ by 1 inch (1.5 × 2.5 cm) under this opening as reinforcement (B2, B3). Now, fold section 2 around (B4) and close the pocket by stitching the second seam.

Stitch a short piece of bias tape to the

ends of the pockets as reinforcement for the fibreglass rods (C). Do this as follows: Stitch a piece of tape 1½ inch (4 cm) long to the sail (C1) and ¼ inch (0.7 cm) away from the bottom edge. Only then can you proceed with the ¼-inch-deep (0.7 cm) hem of the pocket for the fibreglass rod (C2). The tape is placed ⅜ inch (1 cm) into the seam with 1⅛ inch (3 cm) extending beyond the hem

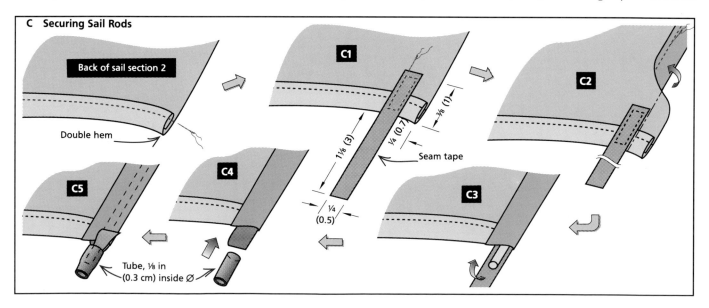

C Securing Sail Rods

Back of sail section 2

Double hem

C1

1⅛ (3)

¼ (0.7)

⅜ (1)

¼ (0.5)

Seam tape

C2

C3

C4

C5

Tube, ⅛ in (0.3 cm) inside ⌀

(C3). No Dacron reinforcement is necessary when sections 2 and 3 are sewn together. The pocket, also ¼ inch (0.7 cm) wide, is created according to instruction B, but without Dacron reinforcement (B5). This opening is later used for the vinyl end cap that holds the stand-off.

You should have finished both halves of the sail before sewing the sleeves for the side bar (made from Dacron). Take the relevant measurement from sketch D. Fold the Dacron tape in half lengthwise before sewing it to the nylon. Push the edge of the nylon ⅜ inches (1 cm) into the Dacron tape. The cut-outs for the side bar connectors are made with the tip of the hot gun. Measurements are found in sketch D. On the right half of the sail, the sleeve is sewn on starting at the top. At the end of the sleeve, you will have two layers of Dacron tape. On the left half of the sail, start at the end of the sleeve. Here, too, use two layers 1⅛ inch (3 cm) each of Dacron and use the zigzag stitch, sewing towards the top. Sew back and forth a few times at the ends of the sleeves.

You can now join both halves together with the seam on the front of the sail, since it will be covered later by the Dacron sleeve. The edges of both sections are flush together and sewn using the French seam (see page 20). The middle bar sleeve consists of 28½-inch-long (71 cm) and 1-inch-wide (2.5 cm)

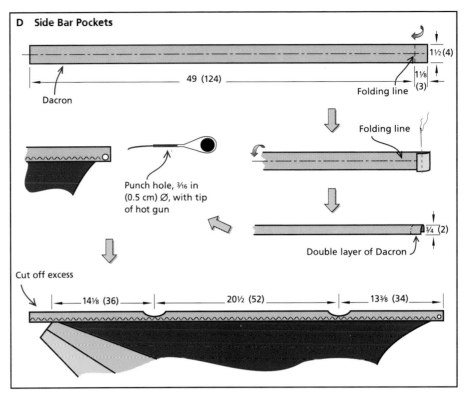

D Side Bar Pockets

Dacron tape. Use the tip of a hot gun to make oval cut-outs. The holes created are used later for the center cross bar and the front spar. The size of the holes are indicated on drawing E1. Start sewing from the top. Two parallel seams attach the sleeve to the sail. On the end, the Dacron will again consist of two layers.

Dacron reinforcement at the tip of the kite prevents the graphite rods from pushing through the cloth. To give additional and stronger support to those rods, stitch an additional piece of protective Dacron over the tip. Remember, however, that this will add weight to the kite. The Bel Air kite here is a light-wind version, so we have not used added reinforcement. Drawing E2 shows how the reinforcement is stitched

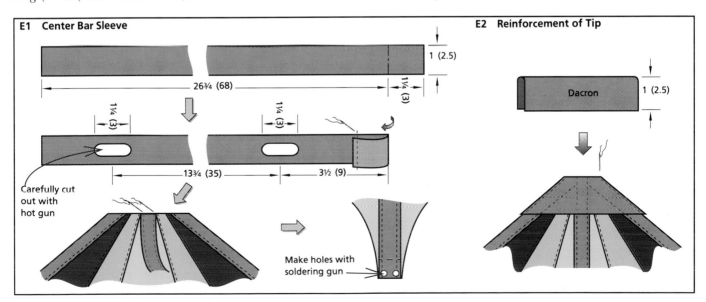

E1 Center Bar Sleeve

E2 Reinforcement of Tip

F Side Bars (4x)

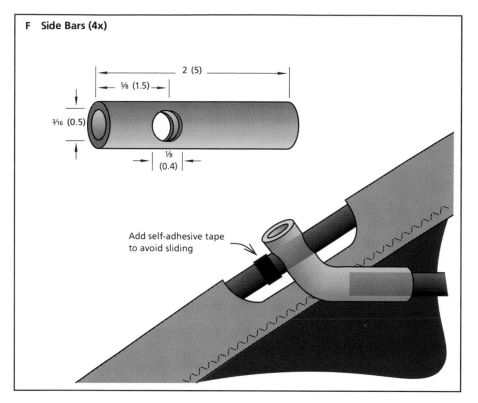

2 (5)

⅝ (1.5)

³⁄₁₆ (0.5)

⅛ (0.4)

Add self-adhesive tape to avoid sliding

to the sail. After the Dacron strip has been sewn to the sail, cut off the excess material on both sides close to the outer seam, as shown in the drawing, with the tip of the hot gun.

Using a fine-tip hot gun, cut small holes through the double-layered Dacron at the end of the sleeves (D and E1). Elastic cords, ¹⁄₁₆ (0.2 cm) ø, are looped through these holes.

You have just finished all the work on the sail. The next step is to prepare the rods for the frame. Side bars are ⅝ inches (1.5 cm) long each. Aluminum connectors join both halves of the frame. Smooth out sharp edges at the end of the rod before inserting them in the connectors. Cut one of the 32½-inch-long (82.5 cm) rods in half. Connect one of these to a 32½-inch-long

(82.5 cm) graphite rod. The ends of the rods are glued into the connector using fast-acting glue. The four T-connectors for the side bar are cut from the ³⁄₁₆ inch (0.5) inside ø hose, see F. Holes, ³⁄₁₆ inch (0.4 cm) ø, are punched through at the end of the connector. Now, push the side bars into the sleeves. The T-connectors are where the cut-outs are. Pushing the rods through the holes, while somewhat difficult, is possible by applying a little pressure. You must construct the center cross before the 27½-inch-long (69 cm) center bar is pushed into the pocket (G). We recommend first pushing the aluminum tube into the hose, then sliding the graphite rod into the sleeve and the hose of the center cross over it. The ends of the graphite rods should be smoothed out with a file; but be careful: the dust is very dangerous! Now, attach the arrow nocks over the end of the rods. A rubber band tightens the sleeve and supports the rod. Next, push the fibreglass rods into the sleeves, starting between sections 2 and 3. For position and measurements, see the pattern diagram.

The rods should extend about 1 inch (2–3 cm) beyond the sleeves. Cut off any excess and smooth the ends with a file. Pull ¼-inch-wide (0.5 cm) seam binding (C) tightly over the fibreglass rod and secure it with a piece of ⅛ inch (0.3 cm) inside ø hose. For this you might also use an end cap of the same size (C4 and C5). The end caps on the

G Center Cross

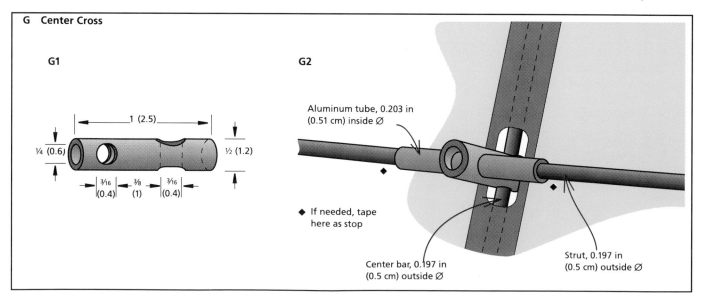

G1

¼ (0.6)

1 (2.5)

½ (1.2)

³⁄₁₆ (0.4)   ⅜ (1)   ³⁄₁₆ (0.4)

G2

Aluminum tube, 0.203 in (0.51 cm) inside ø

◆ If needed, tape here as stop

Center bar, 0.197 in (0.5 cm) outside ø

Strut, 0.197 in (0.5 cm) outside ø

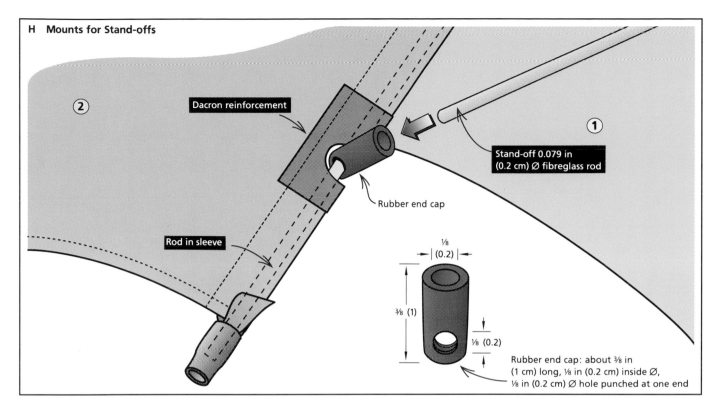

H Mounts for Stand-offs

② Dacron reinforcement

Rod in sleeve

Rubber end cap

① Stand-off 0.079 in (0.2 cm) ⌀ fibreglass rod

⅛ (0.2)

⅜ (1)

⅛ (0.2)

Rubber end cap: about ⅜ in (1 cm) long, ⅛ in (0.2 cm) inside ⌀, ⅛ in (0.2 cm) ⌀ hole punched at one end

rods on sections 1 and 2 are also equipped with rubber bands, ¹⁄₁₆ inch (0.2 cm) inside ⌀. These caps are later used for the stand-offs. Slide the fibreglass rods into the sleeves and push the end caps over them at the Dacron reinforcements. Before sliding the end caps over the rods, punch a small hole, ¹⁄₁₆ inch (0.2 cm), into them (H).

Now you have to attach both rear struts. They are each about 27 inches (68 cm) long. Cut them, however, with a bit of excess so that they can be adjusted later. If the rods are too loose in the hose connectors, the ends have to be covered with tape. If the aluminum connectors do not have stops in the middle, you must provide them by adding tape to the struts, about 1¼ inch (3 cm) from each end. The tape will prevent the struts from sliding. The mounts for the stand-offs on the struts consist of three small sections of hose each: two ⅜ inch (1 cm) long, ³⁄₁₆ inch (0.4 cm) inside ⌀, and one ⅝ inch (1.5 cm) long and ¼ inch (0.6 cm) inside ⌀ (I). The shorter pieces prevent the mount from sliding back and forth on the strut. The hose sections are placed about 7 inches (18 cm) away from the

center cross on the inside of the strut (see pattern). Attach the 7⅞-inch-long (20 cm) stand-offs after you have punched a hole ¹⁄₁₆ inch (0.2 cm) ⌀ into it (I).

Now attach the bridle. Start by connecting the front strut with the middle bar. Both ends are then fastened to the T-connector. The rear bridle between the T-connector and the center cross

also consist of one piece of line. Start with a weaver's knot (see page 16) at the center cross and then attach both ends to the T-connectors. The connection between the front and rear bridles is fastened with an overhead loop (see page 20). Balancing the bridle is done with two aluminum rings, ⅝ inch (1.5 cm) ⌀. The exact measurements are listed in the drawing of the pattern.

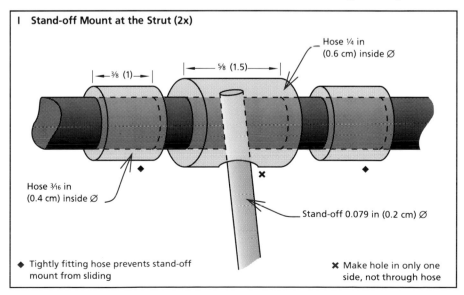

I Stand-off Mount at the Strut (2x)

Hose ¼ in (0.6 cm) inside ⌀

⅜ (1)

⅝ (1.5)

Hose ³⁄₁₆ in (0.4 cm) inside ⌀

Stand-off 0.079 in (0.2 cm) ⌀

◆ Tightly fitting hose prevents stand-off mount from sliding

✕ Make hole in only one side, not through hose

RELAX II

Anyone who enjoys fast kites and kites that can be flown with precision is well served with the Relax II. A similar kite, introduced in the book *The Fantastic World of Kites*, was godfather to the Relax II we present here, a truly high-tech piece of equipment. Like its predecessor, this kite has domed wings and will keep its profile even in low-wind conditions, due to the use of fibreglass rods. In addition, the leading edges are shortened, which makes the kite more maneuverable and faster. Another featured item: two stand-offs each, attached to the left and right sides of the kite, support the front tension of the sail. The concave-shaped trailing edge assures a quiet flight. In addition, a Dacron rope is sewn into the double-folded hem of the trailing edge. The kite moves without making a sound and is particularly fast in tight curves. The bridle adjustments given are designed to accommodate extreme positions in flight; however, they tend to cause the kite to tip over laterally on take-off. But this danger can be overcome if the lines are pulled tight enough; the kite will then become very sensitive and react quickly to your steering maneuvers. The Relax II is designed for winds from between 2 and 5 on the Beaufort scale and, depending on the wind speed, needs a line that will withstand 225 to 265 pounds (100–125 kg) of pressure. For flying in even higher winds, use stronger framing rods than those suggested here.

Building Material

2½ sq yd (2 m²) various color nylon sailcloth, 1⅜ oz/sq yd (45 g/m²)

2½ sq yd (2 m²) cardboard or plywood

1 Dacron binding, 12 ft (360 cm) long, 2 in (5 cm) wide

1 waistband, 4 in (10 cm) long, 1½ in (4 cm) wide

Self-adhesive nylon, at least 1½ × 10 in (4 × 25 cm)

8 graphite rods, 32½ in (82.5 cm) long, 0.278 in (0.69 cm) ∅

1 fibreglass-reinforced rod, 148 in (370 cm) long, 0.079 in (0.2 cm) ∅

3 arrow nocks, 0.278 in (0.69 cm) ∅

1 hose, 9⅝ in (25 cm) long, ¼ in (0.6 cm) inside ∅

1 hose, 2⅜ in (6 cm) long, ⁵⁄₁₆ in (0.8 cm) inside ∅

Pattern

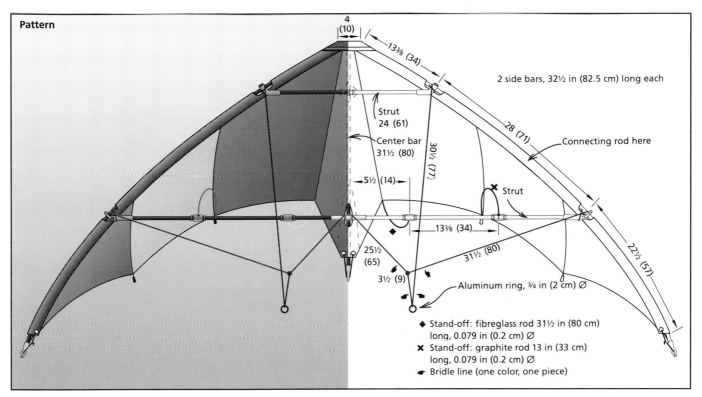

4
(10)

13⅜ (34)

2 side bars, 32½ in (82.5 cm) long each

Strut
24 (61)

Center bar
31½ (80)

28 (71)

Connecting rod here

30½ (77)

5½ (14)

✕ Strut

13⅜ (34)

31½ (80)

22½ (57)

25½
(65)

3½ (9)

Aluminum ring, ¾ in (2 cm) ∅

◆ Stand-off: fibreglass rod 31½ in (80 cm)
long, 0.079 in (0.2 cm) ∅
✕ Stand-off: graphite rod 13 in (33 cm)
long, 0.079 in (0.2 cm) ∅
☛ Bridle line (one color, one piece)

1 hose, 2 in (5 cm) long, 0.197 in
(0.5 cm) inside ∅
1 high-pressure hose, 1⅜ in (3.5 cm)
long, ¼ in (0.6 cm) inside ∅
4 end caps, 0.197 in (0.5 cm) inside ∅
6 end caps, 1⁄16 in (0.2 cm) inside ∅
1 aluminum tube, 3¼ in (8 cm) long,
0.281 in (0.7 cm) ∅ inside
1 binding tape, 14 in (35 cm) long, ³⁄16 in
(0.5 cm) wide
1 elastic cord, 11¾ in (30 cm) long, ⅛ in

(0.3 cm) ∅
4 grommets, ³⁄16 in (0.5 cm) inside ∅
1 grommet, ⁵⁄16 in (0.8 cm) inside ∅
1 nylon string, 12 feet (350 cm) long,
¹⁄32 in (0.1 cm) ∅
1 Dacron line, 20 feet (600 cm) long,
1⁄16 in (0.2 cm) ∅
2 aluminum rings, ¾ in (2 cm) ∅
2 cable connecting tape, ⅛ in (0.3 cm)
wide

Building Instructions

Gather together all the building material you need before starting your project. If there is no kite store in your area, you might order it through the mail or find what you need in hobby or home-improvement shops. Nylon sail-cloth and graphite rods may also be found in shops that make sails for boats and stores selling archery equipment.

∧ Sail Pattern

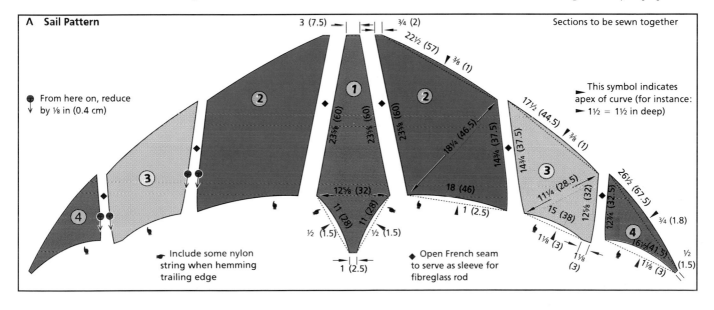

3 (7.5)   ¾ (2)

22½ (57)   ⅜ (1)

Sections to be sewn together

● From here on, reduce
↓ by ⅛ in (0.4 cm)

② ① ②

③

③

④

23⅝ (60)   23⅝ (60)   23⅝ (60)

18¼ (46.5)   14¾ (37.5)

17½ (44.5)   ⅜ (1)

☛ This symbol indicates
apex of curve (for instance:
☛ 1½ = 1½ in deep)

12⅝ (32)

11 (28)   11 (28)

½ (1.5)   ½ (1.5)

18 (46)

1 (2.5)

14¾ (37.5)

11¼ (28.5)

15 (38)   12⅝ (32)

1⅛ (3)   1⅛ (3)

26½ (67.5)

¾ (1.8)

12¼ (32.5)

16¼ (41.5)

½ (1.5)

1⅛ (3)

1 (2.5)

☛ Include some nylon
string when hemming
trailing edge

◆ Open French seam
to serve as sleeve for
fibreglass rod

33

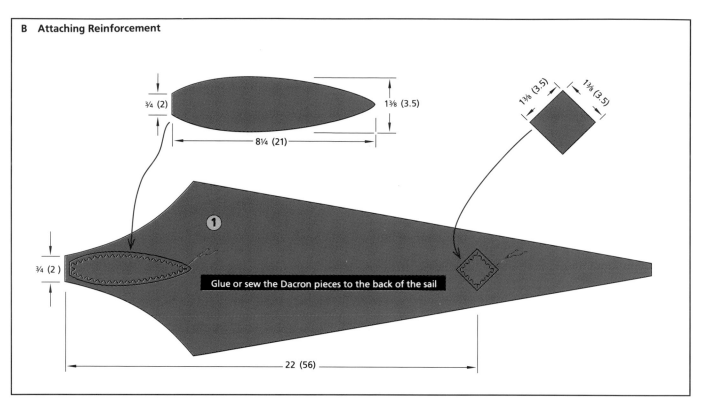

B   Attaching Reinforcement

¾ (2)

1⅜ (3.5)

8¼ (21)

1⅜ (3.5)

1⅜ (3.5)

①

¾ (2)

Glue or sew the Dacron pieces to the back of the sail

22 (56)

The edges 1 to 4 (A) of the individual sail sections are curved; it is therefore essential to first make templates. Trailing edges are marked with arrows (A), indicating the deepest point in the concave curve. The red dots with arrows pointing downwards indicate where the curve begins. At the end point, the material must be reduced by ³⁄₁₆ inch (0.4 cm). (See drawing A and page 20.) First, hem the trailing edges of each section. Sections 1–4 are joined with a French seam. Drawing C shows how to insert a nylon string. Let the nylon extend ⅜ inch (1 cm) beyond the hem on each end. Every seam is treated this way. In addition, section 1 is reinforced on two places with self-adhesive nylon. If this material should not be available, you can also use Dacron material and sew it to the sail. The reinforcement is placed on the back of the sail. In drawing B you can see the position and measurements. After the reinforcements are attached (sewn or glued) to the sail, the lower end is folded towards the back and stitched in place. The nylon string inside the seam is carefully placed in the hem. Fold the end of the string inside the portion that is folded over, so it won't be visible once the hem is finished.

The side-bar sleeves consist of a 2-inch-wide (5 cm) strip of Dacron (E). Before the sleeve is stitched to the edge, it must be evened out with a hot knife. You must establish an even arc. The deepest part of the arc is also the place where the rear strut and side bar join. The tape is folded and sewn to the edge with a zigzag stitch.

At the tip of the wing, the nylon tape has to be sewn carefully to the Dacron sleeve to avoid tearing later. Leave about ½ inch (1 cm) open (E2) where the sections are sewn together. Above that open section, and close to the edge, stitch back and forth a few times so that the fibreglass rod won't poke through the cloth later. At the tip of the wing, you have two layers of material. Here you punch a hole, using the tip of the

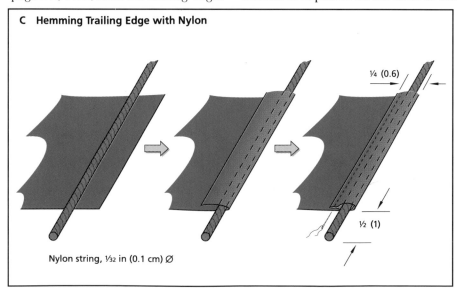

C   Hemming Trailing Edge with Nylon

¼ (0.6)

½ (1)

Nylon string, ¹⁄₃₂ in (0.1 cm) Ø

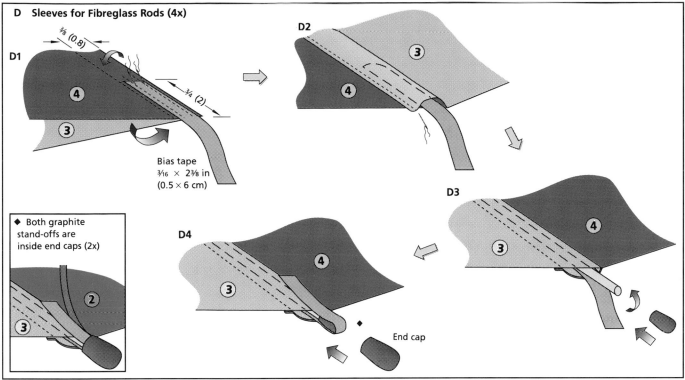

D Sleeves for Fibreglass Rods (4x)

D1

³/₈ (0.8)

④

③

³/₄ (2)

Bias tape
³/₁₆ × 2³/₈ in
(0.5 × 6 cm)

D2

③

④

◆ Both graphite
stand-offs are
inside end caps (2x)

②

③

D4

④

③

End cap

D3

④

③

hot gun. Place a grommet in both of the openings, ³/₁₆ in (0.5 cm) ⌀. Two more grommets are also attached left and right to the center bar (see diagram K).

Now, join all seven sections. Start with section 1 and work towards the outside. Conclude with sewing section 3 to section 4. As you can see in drawing D, the open French seam is used as sleeve for the fibreglass rods. For this reason it is important that the seam is at

least ³/₈ inch (0.8) cm wide. Start sewing the seam at the trailing edge. Make sure that both sections are well lined up. You should have an even transition from one section to the next. Sew the seam with a straight stitch.

The next step is to sew a nylon tape 2³/₈ inches (6 cm) long and ³/₁₆ inch (0.5 cm) wide on the hem of the trailing edge. For reasons of clarity, we did not show the ³/₈ inch (1 cm) excess of the

nylon tape in drawing D1. Both the nylon tape and nylon string have to be carefully scwn in. Cut off any tape extending beyond the ends. As indicated in drawing D2, the seam is folded over and stitched down. Make sure you leave an opening for inserting the ¹/₁₆-in (0.2 cm) ⌀ fibreglass rod.

The reinforcement of the tip is done as before. First, add a layer of Dacron; on top of that sew a piece of strong

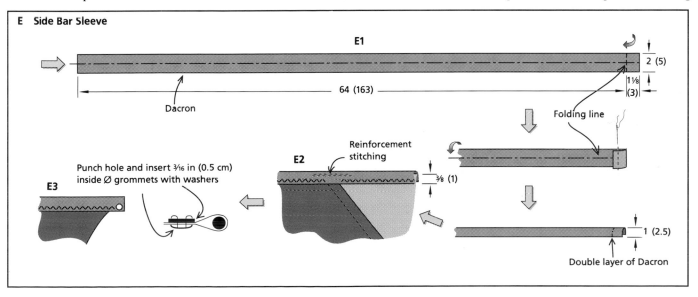

E Side Bar Sleeve

E1

2 (5)

64 (163)

1¹/₈
(3)

Dacron

Folding line

Reinforcement
stitching

E2

³/₈ (1)

1 (2.5)

Double layer of Dacron

Punch hole and insert ³/₁₆ in (0.5 cm)
inside ⌀ grommets with washers

E3

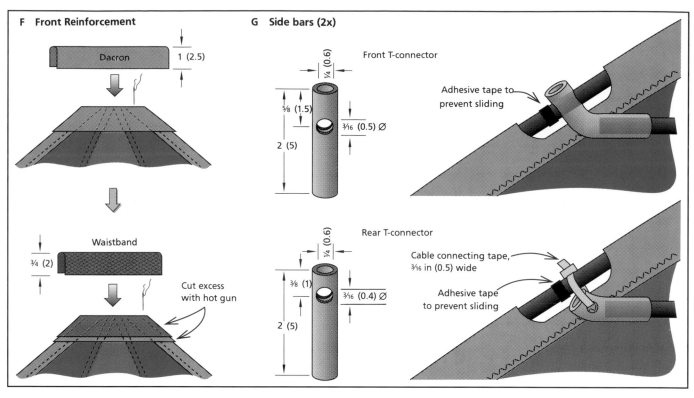

F Front Reinforcement

Dacron 1 (2.5)

Waistband

¾ (2)

Cut excess with hot gun

G Side bars (2x)

Front T-connector

¼ (0.6)

⅝ (1.5) ³⁄₁₆ (0.5) Ø

2 (5)

Adhesive tape to prevent sliding

Rear T-connector

¼ (0.6)

⅜ (1) ³⁄₁₆ (0.4) Ø

2 (5)

Cable connecting tape, ³⁄₁₆ in (0.5) wide

Adhesive tape to prevent sliding

---

waistband. During this procedure, you might have to exchange your sewing-machine needle for a heavier one. Instructions for sewing can be seen in diagram F. Waistband and Dacron are sewn close to the outside edge at the sleeves. Excess material is cut off with the hot knife. This kind of reinforcement will prevent rods from tearing through the material, even if the kite should crash hard onto the ground.

Sewing is now completed. Proceed by preparing the sections needed for the center cross. The center cross consists of a piece of hose ¼ inch (0.6 cm) inside Ø and an aluminum tube serving as connector. Measurements for the hose are given in diagram H. The connector tube is 3 inches (8 cm) long with a ¼ inch (0.7 cm) inside Ø. With the fine tip of a hot gun, make two cut-outs in the reinforcement part of the sail. One

cut-out, at the cross bar, is oval and is 2 inches (5 cm) long. The other cut-out, where the front strut meets the center bar, is round and about ⅜ inch (1 cm) in diameter. Slide the cross bar over the 32-inch-long (80 cm) center bar and place the graphite rod into the sleeve. Cut the rod, a little at a time, until it is the proper length. Now, slip an arrow nock over the end; the sail is stretched with an elastic cord. Side bars are made from two 32½-inch (82.5 cm) graphite rods. Aluminum tubes are used as connectors. Use fast-acting glue to secure the rods in the tubes.

Next, make four T-connectors, each from a 2-inch-long (5 cm) hose (G). With a pointed hot-knife, cut two half-moon shaped holes into each of the sleeves of the side bar—measurements are given in the pattern.

Slide the side bar into the Dacron sleeves. T-connectors are placed at the cut-outs. Use a little bit of pressure when sliding the connector tubes through the hose. Place arrow nocks at the ends of the rods and, again, secure them in place with fast-acting glue.

Elastic cord provides tension and gives the leading edge of the kite the

---

H Center Cross

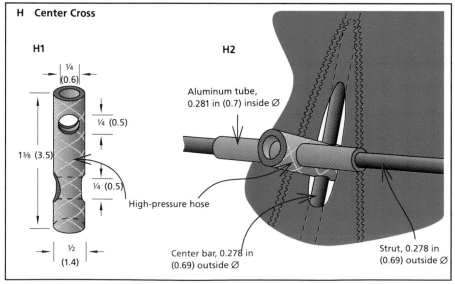

H1

¼ (0.6)

¼ (0.5)

1⅜ (3.5)

¼ (0.5)

½ (1.4)

H2

Aluminum tube, 0.281 in (0.7) inside Ø

High-pressure hose

Center bar, 0.278 in (0.69) outside Ø

Strut, 0.278 in (0.69) outside Ø

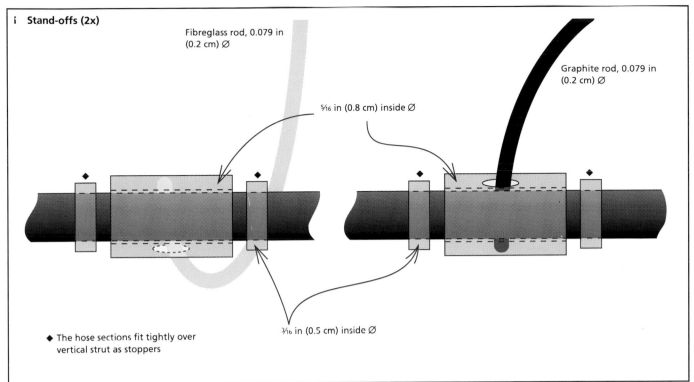

i Stand-offs (2x)

Fibreglass rod, 0.079 in (0.2 cm) Ø

Graphite rod, 0.079 in (0.2 cm) Ø

⁵⁄₁₆ in (0.8 cm) inside Ø

³⁄₁₆ in (0.5 cm) inside Ø

◆ The hose sections fit tightly over vertical strut as stoppers

aerodynamically favorable shape.

Again, step-by-step, shorten the 24½-inch-long (61 cm) front strut. The strut is connected to the center bar at several places. Consider using a ⁵⁄₁₆-inch (0.8 cm) Ø grommet to avoid tearing the material. Very firmly attached to the left and right of each connection are 0.197 in (0.5 cm) Ø hose sections (J). Now, put both rear struts, consisting of two 32-inch-long (80 cm) rods, in place.

The left and right side bars are cut to fit. End caps, ¹⁄₁₆ in (0.2 cm) Ø, are fitted over the ends of the fibreglass rods and inserted in the sleeves. The rods are tightly fitted and covered with ⁵⁄₃₂-inch (0.4 cm) Ø end caps (D3 and D4). Stand-offs, 11¾ inches (30 cm) long, are placed in the end caps (see diagram) and secured in a ⁵⁄₁₆-inch (0.8 cm) inside Ø hose, as illustrated in diagram I. The 32-inch-long (80 cm)

stand-offs run from the tip to the struts, where they are also held in place by a hose ⁵⁄₁₆ inch (0.8 cm) inside Ø. Finally, the bridle is attached to the center rod with a weaver's knot and then tied to the side bars (T-connection) with a round turn with double half hitch.

Note: Do not inhale the dust and/or vapors, when working with graphite and fibreglass-reinforced material and when hot-cutting sailcloth.

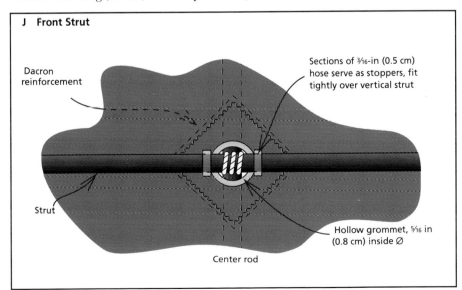

J Front Strut

Dacron reinforcement

Sections of ³⁄₁₆-in (0.5 cm) hose serve as stoppers, fit tightly over vertical strut

Strut

Hollow grommet, ⁵⁄₁₆ in (0.8 cm) inside Ø

Center rod

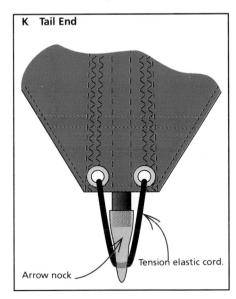

K Tail End

Arrow nock

Tension elastic cord.

SCANNER

In the past, modern stunt kites were usually steered by turning the sail "around" the center rod. Uneven air pressure between the left and the right sides allowed the flier to steer the kite. During WWII, an American named Edward Graber made a very useful discovery. He added a keel at the rear of a modified Eddy kite. The sail surface of this keel was turned forward and, with the help of two steering lines, it could be moved to the left and the right. This ingenious invention allowed Graber to steer the kite; it became a model for the kites used by American marines in training gunners. With the development of stunt kites, an outgrowth of Francis Rogallo's innovative semi-flexible sails, Graber's discovery was more or less forgotten.

The kite presented here is a combination of the Graber and Rogallo kites. The surface of the keel guides the flow of air, which is transferred to the rudder. Semi-flexible sail surfaces provide good lift and allow for precise maneuvering. The kite is designed for flying in a fresh breeze and needs a 200-pound (100 kg) line.

Note: Avoid inhaling the dust you will create when cutting graphite or fibreglass-reinforced rods or the fumes from working with a hot-cutter or soldering gun.

Building Material

- 2½ sq yd (2 m²) various color nylon sailcloth, 1 oz/sq yd (32 g/m²)
- 2 graphite rods, 31 in (78 cm) long, 0.213 in (0.54 cm) ∅
- 5 graphite rods, 32½ in (82.5 cm) long, 0.234 in (0.59 cm) ∅
- 3 graphite rods, 29 in (72.5 cm) long, 0.157 in (0.4 cm) ∅
- 1 graphite rod, 7 in (17 cm) long, 0.157 in (0.4 cm) ∅
- 1 fibreglass-reinforced rod, 16 in (40 cm) long, 0.118 in (0.3 cm) ∅
- 3 arrow nocks, ¼ in (0.59 cm) ∅
- 2 arrow nocks, 5/32 in (0.4 cm) ∅
- 1 arrow nock, 7/32 in (0.54 cm) ∅
- 1 hose, 9½ in (24 cm) long, ¼ in (0.6 cm) inside ∅

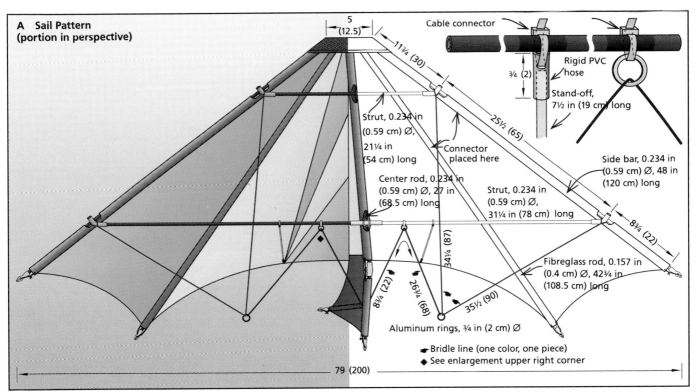

A Sail Pattern
(portion in perspective)

5 (12.5)

11¾ (30)

Cable connector

Rigid PVC hose

¾ (2)

Stand-off, 7½ in (19 cm) long

Strut, 0.234 in (0.59 cm) ∅, 21¼ in (54 cm) long

Connector placed here

25½ (65)

Side bar, 0.234 in (0.59 cm) ∅, 48 in (120 cm) long

Center rod, 0.234 in (0.59 cm) ∅, 27 in (68.5 cm) long

Strut, 0.234 in (0.59 cm) ∅, 31¼ in (78 cm) long

8¾ (22)

34¼ (87)

Fibreglass rod, 0.157 in (0.4 cm) ∅, 42¾ in (108.5 cm) long

8¾ (22)

26¾ (68)

35½ (90)

Aluminum rings, ¾ in (2 cm) ∅

🢒 Bridle line (one color, one piece)
◆ See enlargement upper right corner

79 (200)

---

1 high-pressure hose, 1³⁄₁₆ in (3 cm) long, ¼ in (0.6 cm) inside ∅

1 rigid PVC hose, 1½ in (4 cm) long, 0.118 in (0.3 cm) inside ∅

2 vinyl end caps, ⅛ in (0.3 cm) inside ∅

1 aluminum connector, 3¼ in (8 cm) long, 0.234 in (0.59 cm) inside ∅, with vertical bar

2 aluminum tubes, 0.234 in (0.59 cm) inside ∅

1 V-connector (plastic), 165°, ⁷⁄₃₂ in (0.54 cm) inside ∅

1 Dacron strip, 138 in (350 cm) long, 2 in (5 cm) wide

1 Dacron strip, 94½ in (240 cm) long, ⅝ in (1.5 cm) wide

1 Velcro tape, 3¼ in (8 cm) long, ¾ in (2 cm) wide

1 felt tape, 3¼ in (8 cm) long, ¾ in (2 cm) wide

5 grommets, ³⁄₁₆ in (0.5 cm) inside ∅

1 binding tape, 10 in (25 cm) long, ³⁄₁₆ in (0.5 cm) wide

2 aluminum rings, ⅝ in (1.5 cm) ∅

2 aluminum rings, ¾ in (2 cm) ∅

4 cable connecting tapes, ⅛ in (0.3 cm) wide

2 cable connecting tapes, ³⁄₁₆ in (0.5 cm) wide

1 elastic cord, 27½ in (70 cm) long, ⅛ in (0.3 cm) ∅

1 waistband, 8 in (20 cm) long, ⅛ in (0.3 cm) wide

1 Dacron line, 10 yd (900 cm) long, ¹⁄₃₂ in (0.1 cm) ∅

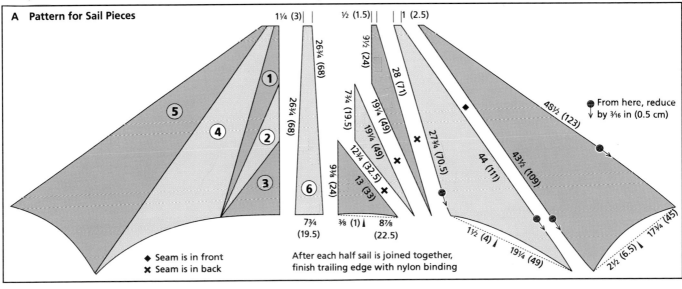

A Pattern for Sail Pieces

1¼ (3)   ½ (1.5)   1 (2.5)

26¾ (68)

26¾ (68)

9½ (24)

28 (71)

7¾ (19.5)

19¼ (49)

19¼ (49)

12¾ (32.5)

13 (33)

27¾ (70.5)

48½ (123)

● From here, reduce ↓ by ³⁄₁₆ in (0.5 cm)

44 (111)

43½ (109)

9⅜ (24)

7¾ (19.5)

⅜ (1)   8⅞ (22.5)

1½ (4)   19¼ (49)

2½ (6.5)   17¾ (45)

◆ Seam is in front
✗ Seam is in back

After each half sail is joined together, finish trailing edge with nylon binding

39

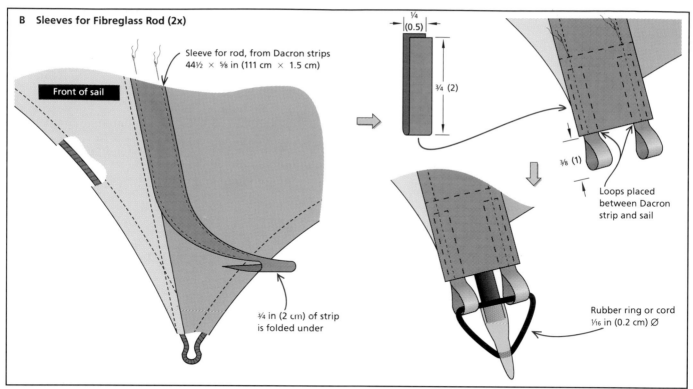

B Sleeves for Fibreglass Rod (2x)

Front of sail

Sleeve for rod, from Dacron strips
44½ × ⅝ in (111 cm × 1.5 cm)

¼ (0.5)

¾ (2)

⅜ (1)

Loops placed
between Dacron
strip and sail

¾ in (2 cm) of strip
is folded under

Rubber ring or cord
1/16 in (0.2 cm) Ø

Building Instructions

Building the Scanner requires a certain amount of skill in the use of a sewing machine, but all necessary techniques are described step-by-step and are easy to follow.

Start by cutting out all twelve sections of the sail (A). Take note of the curved trailing edges, as well as the slightly curved edges of sections 4 and

5. First sew together sections 1, 2, and 3. Then proceed to sew section 4 to section 1. The seams are on the back. Now, sew section 4 to section 5 in such a way that the seam is in front. Follow these steps for both halves of the sail.

In order to prevent excessive fluttering of the trailing edge, finish the hem with Dacron tape (see also page 34). Make sure that the seam is in the back. Stitch a ⅝-inch-wide (1.5 cm)

Dacron strip over the seams of sections 4 and 5; they serve as sleeves for the fibreglass rods. Prepare a strip 44½ inches (111 cm) long and stitch it to both halves of the sail as shown in diagram B. At the heel, the material is folded over to the inside; two loops, 2 inches (5 cm) wide, are sewn into the Dacron strip (B). The loops should extend about ⅜ inch (1 cm) beyond the sleeve. The end of the sleeve is flush with the

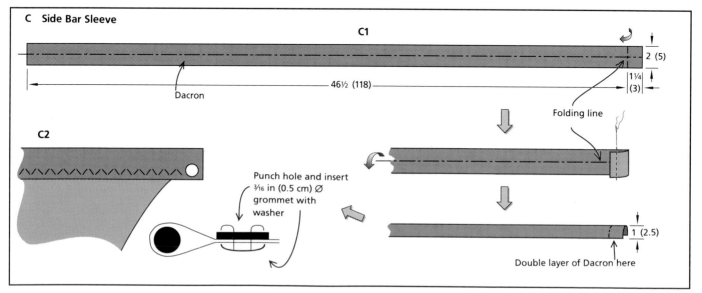

C Side Bar Sleeve

C1

Dacron

46½ (118)

2 (5)

1¼ (3)

Folding line

C2

Punch hole and insert
3/16 in (0.5 cm) Ø
grommet with
washer

Double layer of Dacron here

1 (2.5)

hem of the trailing edge. Next, stitch the sleeve for the fibreglass rod in sandwich fashion at the outside edge of the sail (C). For this, you need to prepare a 48½-inch-long (121 cm) Dacron strip, 2 inches (5 cm) wide. Fold the strip in half lengthwise. Start at the tip and use the zigzag stitch. Place the sail ⅜ inch (1 cm) deep into the Dacron sleeve and stitch (C2). On the bottom, fold 1¼ inch (3 cm) of the material under and stitch carefully (several times back and forth). Do the same with the other half of the sail.

The keel is made from section 6 (see A). First, make a double hem on the short end. Then, fold the nylon lengthwise in half (D). The center bar sleeve, like the side-bar sleeve, is made from a 2-inch-wide (5 cm) Dacron strip. The Dacron is also folded in half lengthwise and placed over the folded nylon piece, overlapping by ⅜ inch (1 cm) (D). Now, the Dacron sleeve and the nylon are sewn together, using the zigzag stitch (D). For extra strength, the Dacron material is folded double at the end. Be absolutely sure that the Dacron sleeve is flush with the hem of the trailing edge.

Now, join the keel sleeve and both halves of the sail. Place the sleeve between both halves (E). If this proves difficult, you can do it in two steps:
1. Stitch the keel sleeve to the left half of the sail.
2. Join the right half and the left half together.

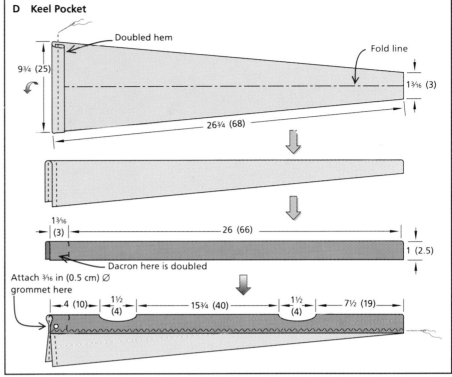

D Keel Pocket

Either way, make sure that the seam is on the back of the sail, and that all three layers are flush with the trailing edge, where the seam— because of the carefully sewn-in reinforcement binding—is safely stitched in place. In diagram E2, you can see that the hem is to be turned under and stitched to one half of the sail.

With a hot gun, make two holes ³⁄₁₆ inch (0.5 cm) ∅ in the reinforced ends of each of the end and side-bar sleeves. Attach a ³⁄₁₆ (0.5 cm) ∅ grommet in each hole (see diagrams C and I). Also, using the hot gun or cutter, remove a section in the center and side-bar sleeve for the T- and cross connector. Measurements are listed in the sail pattern diagram and sketch D. Make sure that you do not inhale the vapors created when hot-cutting the Dacron material; it is hazardous.

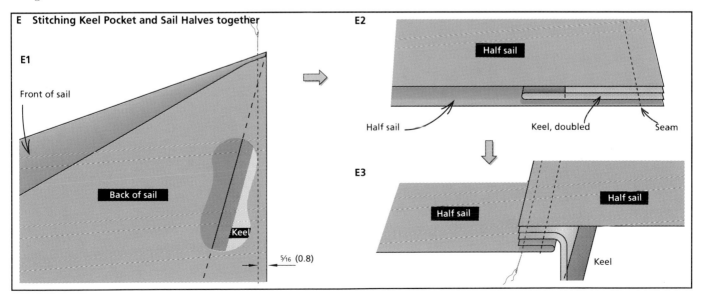

E Stitching Keel Pocket and Sail Halves together

F Nose Reinforcement

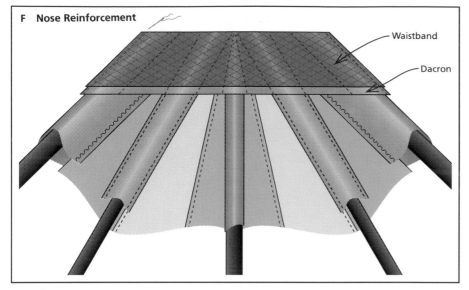

Waistband

Dacron

The nose of the Scanner is reinforced with a layer of Dacron as well as a piece of waistband; see diagram F. First put the Dacron over the front edge. The material in the vicinity of the center bar must become slightly domed. Stitch along the side center and fibreglass rod sleeve (see sketch F). Excess material is carefully cut off, making sure that the sleeves are not damaged. Now, fold the waistband lengthwise down the middle, place it also over the Dacron, and stitch everything together very carefully. Stitch another seam close to the side-bar sleeve. Excess waistband is also cut off.

Next, make the four T-connectors, using ¼-inch (0.6 cm) inside ⌀ hose, and a cross connector, using 1³⁄₁₆-inch-long (3 cm) high-pressure hose with ¼ inch (0.6 cm) inside ⌀. Cut a graphite rod, 0.234 inch (0.59 cm) ⌀, in half.

Connect both pieces to a graphite rod, 32½ inches (82.5 cm) long and 0.234 inch (0.59 cm) ⌀, using aluminum tubes. Slide both side bars into their respective sleeves. T-connectors are placed at the cut-offs (see also sail pattern). Some pressure is necessary to push the hose through the tube.

Place both sail rods, 28½ inches (72.5 cm) long and 0.157 inch (0.4 cm) ⌀, into their respective sleeves. Like the side bars, the sail rods consist of one and a half pieces, but they are joined at their blunt ends. Arrow nocks are placed at each end and the fibreglass bar is secured with elastic cord.

Next, slide the center bar, consisting of a graphite rod 27 inches (68.5 cm) long and 0.213 inch (0.54 cm) ⌀, into the sleeve. The cross connector is placed at the cut-off, which is made from high-pressure hose (H).

Now, make the front strut using a graphite rod 0.213 inch (0.54 cm) in ⌀. The rear strut, graphite rod 0.234 inch (0.59 cm) ⌀, consists of two equally long pieces (see sail pattern). They are pushed into the T-connector as well as in the 3¼-inch-long (8 cm) aluminum connector. This aluminum connector,

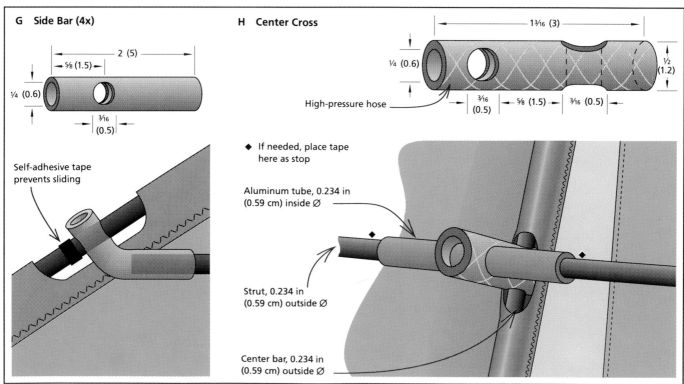

G Side Bar (4x)

2 (5)

⅝ (1.5)

¼ (0.6)

³⁄₁₆ (0.5)

Self-adhesive tape prevents sliding

H Center Cross

1³⁄₁₆ (3)

¼ (0.6)

½ (1.2)

High-pressure hose

³⁄₁₆ (0.5)   ⅝ (1.5)   ³⁄₁₆ (0.5)

◆ If needed, place tape here as stop

Aluminum tube, 0.234 in (0.59 cm) inside ⌀

Strut, 0.234 in (0.59 cm) outside ⌀

Center bar, 0.234 in (0.59 cm) outside ⌀

preferably, should have a center bar to prevent the struts from moving. If there is no center bar, you must provide both strut bars with a sufficiently thick layer of fibreglass-reinforced tape about 1½ inches (4 cm) from the ends.

Both stand-offs are made from fibreglass rods 0.118 inch (0.3 cm) ⌀. At the trailing edge of the left and right half of the sail each, attach a vinyl cap ⅛ inch (0.3 cm) inside ⌀ fastened into place with a narrow cable fastener. Punch a hole with the fine tip of a hot gun into the right and left trailing edges—making sure that the seam is not damaged. The positions of the holes are between parts 1 and 4 (see drawing A). Punch a hole ³⁄₃₂ inch (0.2 cm) ⌀ into the very end of the end caps and fasten them to the trailing edge with the cable fastener that must be guided around the Dacron reinforcement.

The stand-offs at the rear struts are placed into rigid PVC-hose, 0.118 inch (0.3 cm) inside ⌀. Holes are punched at the very end of the ¾-inch-long (2 cm) hose and fastened to the strut with cable fastener (see sail pattern). It is recommended that you place adhesive tape under the cable fastener to prevent it from sliding. Position the 7½-inch-long (19 cm) rod into the support.

If you want to use the Scanner without a keel, you must secure the center bar with an arrow nock and elastic cord. The bridle is not guided through the ring to the keel but rather attached to the center cross (see sail pattern). If, however, the kite is to be used with a keel, you must stitch a strip of Velcro tape about ¾ inches (2 cm) long along the rear edge of the keel. Cut out the keel (section 7) according to drawing J. Edges J1 and J2 are hemmed with a double seam. Carefully stitch a ¾-inch-wide (2 cm) felt strip to edge J1. Following diagram I, stitch a ¾-inch-wide (2 cm) piece of Dacron to one side of the sail, folding it over before sewing it in place, and you will have made a loop.

The hemmed edge serves as a sleeve: fold a 2-inch-wide (5 cm) piece of Dacron, sewing it—as already demonstrated—to the keel in sandwich fashion. For reinforcement, fold 2 inches (5 cm) of the material under at

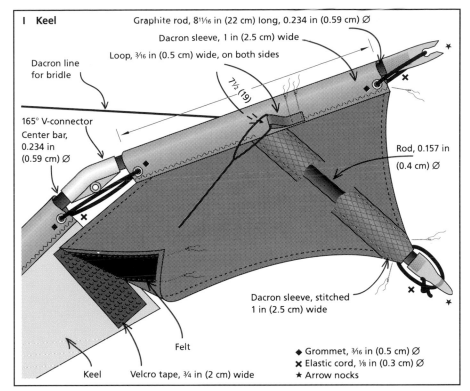

I Keel

Graphite rod, 8¹¹⁄₁₆ in (22 cm) long, 0.234 in (0.59 cm) ⌀
Dacron sleeve, 1 in (2.5 cm) wide
Loop, ³⁄₁₆ in (0.5 cm) wide, on both sides
Dacron line for bridle
165° V-connector
Center bar, 0.234 in (0.59 cm) ⌀
7½ (19)
Rod, 0.157 in (0.4 cm) ⌀
Dacron sleeve, stitched 1 in (2.5 cm) wide
Felt
Keel
Velcro tape, ¾ in (2 cm) wide

◆ Grommet, ³⁄₁₆ in (0.5 cm) ⌀
✕ Elastic cord, ⅛ in (0.3 cm) ⌀
★ Arrow nocks

each end. Leave the seam open where the pocket slides under the Dacron sleeve (I). Next, stitch two small loops of 2-inch-wide (5 cm) tape to the left and right from the sleeve (I).

Fasten two grommets at the end of the Dacron sleeve of the keel. Slide a graphite rod, 8⅝ inch (22 cm) long and ⁷⁄₃₂ inches (0.54 cm) in ⌀, into the sleeve and connect it to the 165° V-connector of the center bar. Two rubber bands will

stretch the sail. One rod, 0.157 inch (0.4 cm) ⌀, with an arrow nock and elastic cord stretches the keel to the back (I). Push the Velcro together securely to tighten the sail of the rudder. Attach the bridle line as instructed on the sail pattern. A line, running to the center bar, is attached to the left and right to the keel. Two aluminum rings are used to attach the bridle line and to change the angle of inclination.

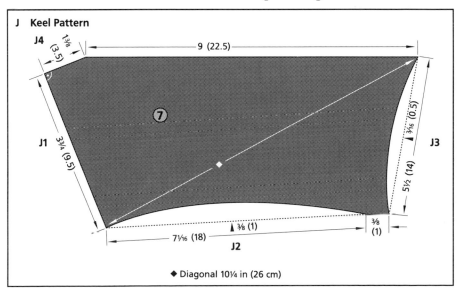

J Keel Pattern

J4
1³⁄₈ (3.5)
9 (22.5)
⑦
J1
3¾ (9.5)
J3
³⁄₁₆ (0.5)
5½ (14)
7¹⁄₁₆ (18)
⅜ (1)
³⁄₈ (1)
J2

◆ Diagonal 10¼ in (26 cm)

HEAVY DUTY

It takes strength and skill to maneuver the Heavy Duty. Even with a light breeze it can develop a heavy pull. This kite was designed for wind speed of 2.5 to 4 on the Beaufort scale. If you fly your kite in high wind, it can give your muscles a real workout—hence the name Heavy Duty.

In spite of the about 1⅕-square-yard (1 m²) sail surface, this kite is not sluggish. Tight turns and terrific loops are easy to perform; and only if the flier is in less than good condition will the fun be spoiled.

The frame is almost totally built with graphite rods that are 0.307 inch (0.78 cm) in diameter. Such a frame guarantees good strong flying abilities and a long life. A smooth, straight flight is

ensured by the keel that runs along the center rod and by the winglets that are attached to the sides. Just like the keel, the winglets serve as stabilizers for the sail. In spite of the expansive trailing edge, this kite remains silent even in very tight turns. The trailing edge is domed in strategic places and hemmed with binding tape. The bridle connects on five different points, guaranteeing good distribution of weight.

Only experienced kite builders should attempt to construct this kite. However, the following step-by-step instructions give a very detailed picture of the work to be done. For flying this kite, a flying line of at least 250 pounds (120 kg) strength is recommended.

Note: Do not inhale the dust from

working with graphite and fibreglass-reinforced material or the vapors when hot-cutting sailcloth; it is hazardous to your health.

Building Material

2⅖ sq yd (2 m²) various color nylon sailcloth, 1⅝ oz/sq yd (55 g/m²)

2⅖ sq yd (2 m²) cardboard or plywood

2 graphite rods, 60 in (150 cm) long, 0.307 in (0.78 cm) ∅ for side bars

2 graphite rods, 44½ in (111 cm) long, 0.307 in (0.78 cm) ∅ for rear struts

1 graphite rod, 53¼ in (133 cm) long, 0.307 in (0.78 cm) ∅ for center rod

1 graphite rod, 37 in (92 cm) long, 0.234 in (0.59 cm) ∅ for front struts

Pattern (portion in perspective)

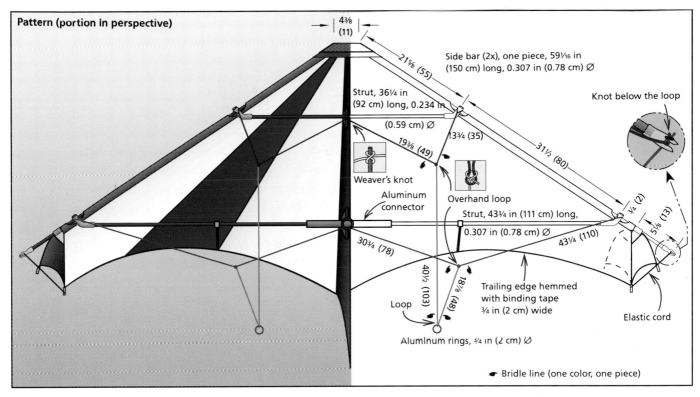

4⅜ (11)

Side bar (2x), one piece, 59¹/₁₆ in (150 cm) long, 0.307 in (0.78 cm) Ø

21⅝ (55)

Strut, 36¼ in (92 cm) long, 0.234 in (0.59 cm) Ø

13¾ (35)

Knot below the loop

19⅜ (49)

31½ (80)

Weaver's knot

Aluminum connector

Overhand loop

Strut, 43¾ in (111 cm) long, 0.307 in (0.78 cm) Ø

¾ (2)

¾ (2)

5⅛ (13)

30¾ (78)

43¼ (110)

40½ (103)

18⅞ (48)

Trailing edge hemmed with binding tape ¾ in (2 cm) wide

Elastic cord

Loop

Aluminum rings, ¾ in (2 cm) Ø

☛ Bridle line (one color, one piece)

2 fibreglass winglet rods, 14 in (35 cm) long, 0.079 in (0.2 cm) Ø for struts

2 fibreglass winglet rods, 9¼ in (23 cm) long, 0.118 in (0.3 cm) Ø for struts

2 fibreglass center bar, 11 in (27.5 cm) long, 0.189 in (0.49 cm) Ø for stand-offs

1 hose, 11¾ in (30 cm) long, ⁵/₁₆ in (0.8 cm) inside Ø

1 hard-plastic PVC hose 3¼ in (8 cm) long, 0.315 in (0.8 cm) outside Ø,

0.234 in (0.59 cm) inside Ø

1 high-pressure hose, 1½ in (4 cm) long, ⅜ in (0.9 cm) inside Ø

4 sections of hose, ⅝ in (1.5 cm) long, ³/₁₆ in (0.5 cm) inside Ø for stand-offs

4 sections of hose, ⅝ in (1.5 cm) long, ⅛ in (0.35 cm) inside Ø for winglets

2 sections of hose, ⅝ in (1.5 cm) long, ⁵/₃₂ in (0.4 cm) inside Ø for winglets

3 arrow nocks, ⁵/₁₆ in (0.78 cm) inside Ø

2 arrow nocks, ⅛ in (0.3 cm) inside Ø

1 Dacron strip, 3¾ yd (340 cm) long, 2 in (5 cm) wide

1 waistband, 8 in (20 cm) long, 2 in (5 cm) wide

binding tape, 106½ in (270 cm) long, ¾ in (2 cm) wide

binding tape, 11¾ in (30 cm) long, ³/₁₆ in (0.5 cm) wide

4 cable binders, ⅛ in (0.3 cm) wide

1 Dacron line, 4 in (10 cm) long, ¹/₁₆ in (0.2 cm) Ø

A Sail Pattern

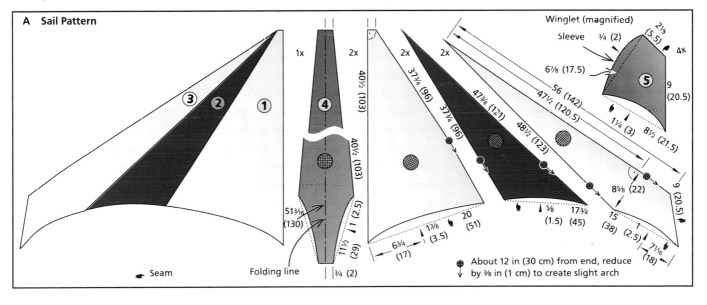

③ ② ①

1x

④

2x

40½ (103)

40½ (103)

51³/₁₆ (130)

11½ (29)

1 (2.5)

¾ (2)

2x

6¾ (17)

1⅜ (3.5)

20 (51)

2x

37¾ (96)

37¾ (96)

⅝ (1.5)

17¾ (45)

2x

47¾ (121)

48½ (123)

47½ (120.5)

56 (142)

Winglet (magnified)

Sleeve ¾ (2)

2⅛ (5.5)

6⅞ (17.5)

⑤

4x

9 (20.5)

1¼ (3)

8½ (21.5)

8⅝ (22)

9 (20.5)

15 (38)

1 (2.5)

7¹/₁₆ (18)

☛ Seam

Folding line

● About 12 in (30 cm) from end, reduce ↓ by ⅜ in (1 cm) to create slight arch

45

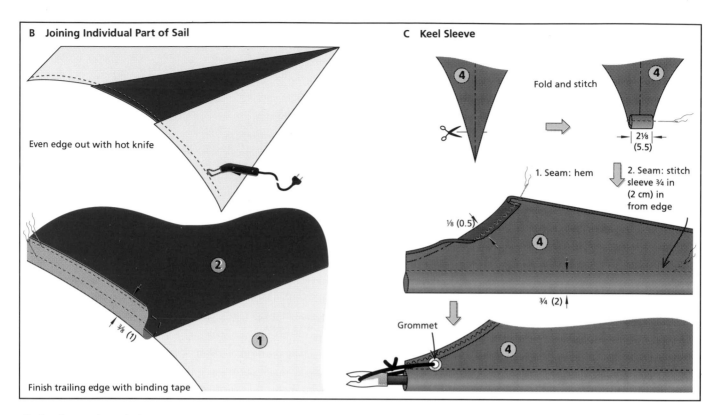

B Joining Individual Part of Sail

Even edge out with hot knife

②

①

⅜ (1)

Finish trailing edge with binding tape

C Keel Sleeve

④

Fold and stitch

④

2⅛ (5.5)

1. Seam: hem

2. Seam: stitch sleeve ¾ in (2 cm) in from edge

⅛ (0.5)

④

¾ (2)

Grommet

④

---

2 aluminum rings, ¾ in (2 cm) ⌀
1 aluminum tube, 3¼ in (8 cm) long,
   0.315 in (0.8 cm) inside ⌀
3 grommets with washer, ³⁄₁₆ in (0.5 cm) ⌀
1 elastic band, ⅛ in (0.3 cm) ⌀

Building Instructions

Since all edges of the Heavy Duty are hemmed you can cut out the pattern with scissors. Cut two of sections 1, 2, and 3 (A), section 4 only once. Also, notice that the edges of sections 1, 2, and 3 have slightly rounded corners that will give the sail a slight arch, which improves the lift-off. In addition, it also increases the tension of the trailing edge, eliminating noise in flight. The shape of the concave edges can be seen in sketch A. The deepest point of the arch is marked by arrows: in other words, not necessarily in the middle.

First, join sections 1, 2 and 3 with French seams (see sketch B). The seams are on the back. Use a hot gun to even out the trailing edge. Then hem the trailing edge with binding tape ¾ inch (2 cm) wide. Cut the binding tape to proper length, fold it lengthwise in half and place over the trailing edge. Now stitch the binding tape with 2 seams to the trailing edge. The bottom tip of keel, section 4, is folded over and stitched as shown in diagram (C). Fold the keel lengthwise in half. The 11½-inch (29 cm) edge of section 4 (A), which consists now of two layers, is sewn together. The center bar sleeve of the keel runs ¾ inch (2 cm) inside the edge. Stitch at a distance of ¾ inch (2 cm) along the side that was originally 51³⁄₁₆ inches (130 cm) long (A). Both halves of the sail and the keel should now be finished.

Joining these three sections requires some skill. Start from the bottom. Place the edges flush on top of each other and stitch them together. It is also possible to break this step down in two phases: first join the keel with one half

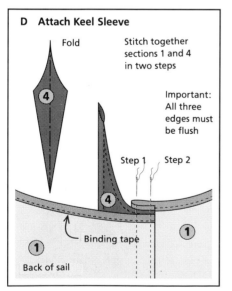

D Attach Keel Sleeve

Fold

Stitch together sections 1 and 4 in two steps

④

Important: All three edges must be flush

Step 1   Step 2

④

Binding tape

①

①

①

Back of sail

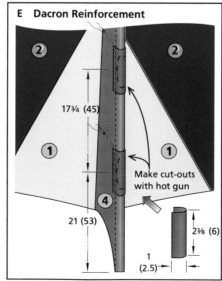

E Dacron Reinforcement

②   ②

①   ①

17¾ (45)

21 (53)

④

Make cut-outs with hot gun

2⅜ (6)

1 (2.5)

46

F Side Bar Sleeve

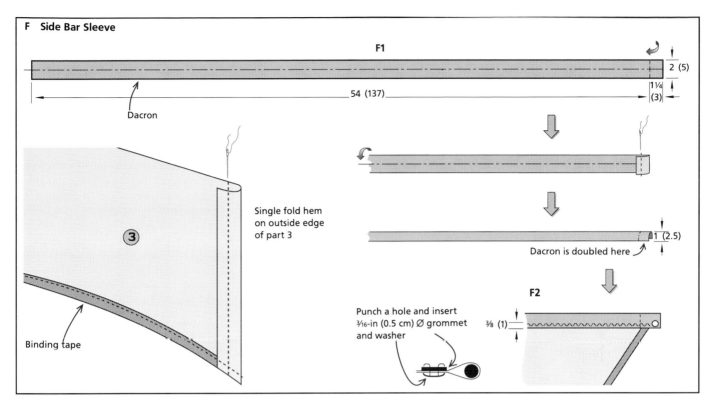

F1

2 (5)

54 (137)

1¼ (3)

Dacron

Single fold hem on outside edge of part 3

③

Binding tape

Dacron is doubled here

1 (2.5)

Punch a hole and insert
³⁄₁₆-in (0.5 cm) Ø grommet
and washer

F2

³⁄₈ (1)

---

of the sail and then add the second half to those already stitched together. In any case, the hem must be turned under and stitched in place (see also diagram D). The center rod sleeve is reinforced with two pieces of Dacron cloth. Fold the 2 × 2⅜-inch (5 × 6 cm) pieces in the middle and stitch over the keel. Measurements are listed in diagram E. The struts are later placed in the cut-outs. Next, hem the short outer side (F). The winglets are being attached on the edge of section 3. The 1¼-inch (3 cm) hem should be on the back of the sail.

The side-bar sleeves are made from 2-inch-wide (5 cm) Dacron webbing folded in half lengthwise. Pull the fold over the edge of a tabletop a few times to set the crease. At the bottom of the sleeve, make a 1¼-inch (3 cm) hem.

Using a zigzag stitch, start sewing from the bottom upwards (see sketch F). Set the width of the stitch on the sewing machine at about ¼ inch (0.6 cm) and the distance between stitches at about ⅛ inch (0.35 cm). After the sleeves have been sewn to both side sections, make cut-outs with the hot gun for the connectors.

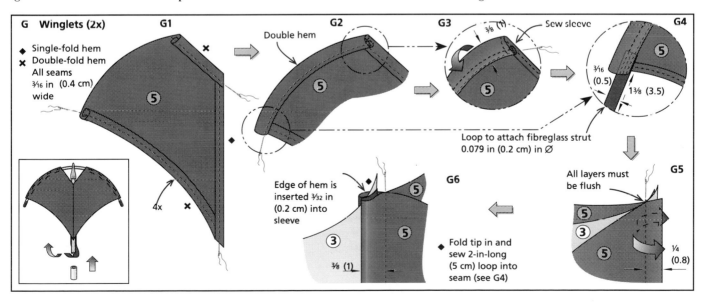

G Winglets (2x)

G1

◆ Single-fold hem
✕ Double-fold hem
All seams
³⁄₁₆ in (0.4 cm)
wide

⑤

4x ✕

G2

Double hem

⑤

G3

³⁄₈ (1)

Sew sleeve

⑤

G4

⑤

³⁄₁₆ (0.5)

1⅜ (3.5)

Loop to attach fibreglass strut
0.079 in (0.2 cm) in Ø

Edge of hem is inserted ³⁄₃₂ in (0.2 cm) into sleeve

G6

⑤

⑤

③

³⁄₈ (1)

◆ Fold tip in and sew 2-in-long (5 cm) loop into seam (see G4)

All layers must be flush

G5

⑤

③

⑤

¼ (0.8)

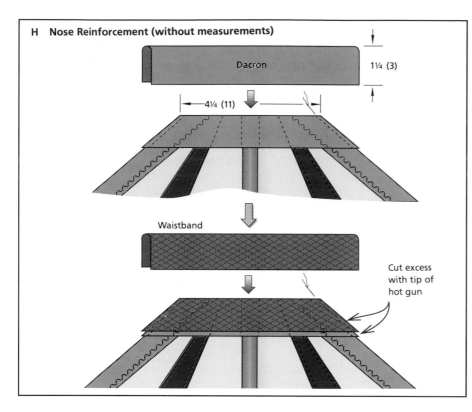

H Nose Reinforcement (without measurements)

Dacron

1¼ (3)

4¼ (11)

Waistband

Cut excess with tip of hot gun

Winglets consist of two symmetrical halves (pattern A). It is best to make a cardboard template first. Then follow the instructions given in diagram G. Start with the single and double-fold hem (G1). The convex-curved edge has a single-fold hem and is where the hem for the sleeve will later be sewn (G2 and G3). Add a 2-inch-wide (5 cm) binding tape to both ends of the sleeve (G5), with ⅝ inch (1.5 cm) of the tape sewn into the seam. This loop later serves as fastener for the strut. You need four winglet halves. These halves are sewn onto the wing ends as sleeves.

Start at the bottom with the seam. Section 3 is now between the winglet halves (G5). Now, fold both halves over and, with an additional seam alongside, close the pocket. The edges of the sec-

tions are inside the sleeve and invisible (G6). You need to sew in a 2-inch-wide (5 cm) piece of binding tape at the end of this sleeve (see also G4).

The tip of the Heavy Duty must be particularly well protected. A layer of folded Dacron is placed over the tip and stitched as illustrated in H. Fold a piece of waistband and sew over the Dacron.

The sewing part of the kite is now completed. The next step is to make T-connectors from four pieces of hose (I). The T-connector for the front strut needs an additional hose, ⁵⁄₁₆ inch (0.8 cm) outside Ø, which is pushed into the connector as support for the front strut. With a hot gun make a hole into each of the ends of the side-bar and center-bar sleeves. Place ³⁄₁₆-inch (0.5 cm) Ø grommets into these holes. Now slide the 60-inch (150 cm) side bars into these sleeves with the T-connectors resting in the cut-outs.

The center cross consists of a 1½-inch-long (4 cm) piece of high-pressure hose (J) and an aluminum tube. Punch a hole into the hose and insert the connector. Next, slide the 52⅜-inch-long (133 cm) center bar into the keel sleeve, with the T-connector resting in the cut-outs.

Next, cut two pieces of hose, ⅝ inch (1.5 cm) long and ⁵⁄₁₆ inch (0.8 cm) inside Ø. Cut an asymmetrical ⅛-inch (0.2 cm) Ø hole through each piece of hose (K). Slide a hose over each side bar.

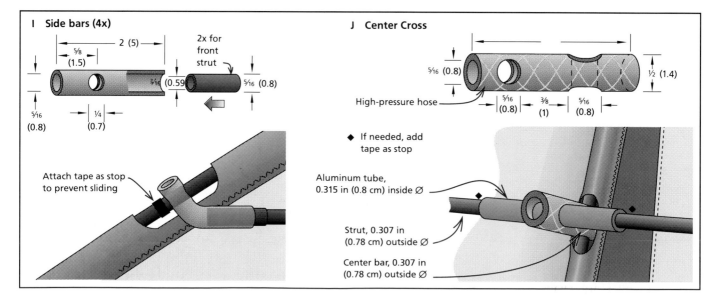

I Side bars (4x)

2 (5)

⅝ (1.5)

2x for front strut

³⁄₁₆ (0.59)

⁵⁄₁₆ (0.8)

⁵⁄₁₆ (0.8)

¼ (0.7)

Attach tape as stop to prevent sliding

J Center Cross

⁵⁄₁₆ (0.8)

½ (1.4)

High-pressure hose

⁵⁄₁₆ (0.8)   ⅜ (1)   ⁵⁄₁₆ (0.8)

◆ If needed, add tape as stop

Aluminum tube, 0.315 in (0.8 cm) inside Ø

Strut, 0.307 in (0.78 cm) outside Ø

Center bar, 0.307 in (0.78 cm) outside Ø

Arrow nocks are used to tighten the sleeves. Place the three aluminum tips, together with the nocks, over the side and center bars. Fasten them with fast-acting glue. Tighten the pockets with elastic cord.

The 14-inch (35 cm) struts of the winglets have a 0.079 inch (0.2 cm) ⌀. The rods are placed into the pockets and secured with a piece of binding tape and piece of hose (K). The vertical fibreglass rod tightens the ends of the wings as well as the stabilizer. Slide the rods into the sleeves with small arrow nocks placed on the ends. Wind a little tape around the ends of the fibreglass rods to give the nocks a tight fit. As illustrated in diagram K, the nocks are positioned next to the hose. With the aid of the sewn-in binding tape and a piece of hose secure the rods at the bottom of the sleeve. Attach a rubber band to this hose. The stabilizer is fastened to the side bar with elastic cord. The elastic cord is located underneath the arrow nock already in place (see sail pattern).

Both stand-offs are made from fibreglass rods 0.189 inch (0.49 cm) ⌀. Punch two small holes into each of the rods exactly where sections 1 and 2 are sewn together. With the aid of narrow binding tape, the pieces of ⅜-inch (0.5 cm) inside ⌀ hose are fastened through the holes as well as tied to the strut (L). Next, prepare 10¾-inch-long (27.5 cm) fibreglass rods and slide them into the

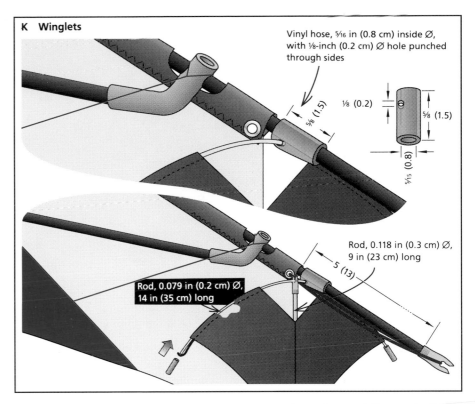

K Winglets

Vinyl hose, 5⁄16 in (0.8 cm) inside ⌀, with ⅛-inch (0.2 cm) ⌀ hole punched through sides

⅝ (1.5)

⅛ (0.2)

⅝ (1.5)

5⁄15 (0.8)

Rod, 0.118 in (0.3 cm) ⌀, 9 in (23 cm) long

5 (13)

Rod, 0.079 in (0.2 cm) ⌀, 14 in (35 cm) long

hose. The kite sail should be pre-tightened, but not too strongly.

The bridle of the kite consists of four sections (see sail pattern). First, fasten the front part of the bridle. Start with a weaver's knot, connecting the center bar and the front strut. The ends of the line are fastened to the right and left side bars. The rear bridle line is connected in the same way: with a

weaver's knot fastened first to the cross bar and then to the T-connector at the side bar (see sail pattern). The front and the rear bridle are connected with one line each. A ¾-inch (2 cm) ⌀ aluminum ring is connected via a loop to the line.

Note: Be careful working with synthetic materials. The slivers, dust, and vapors are hazardous.

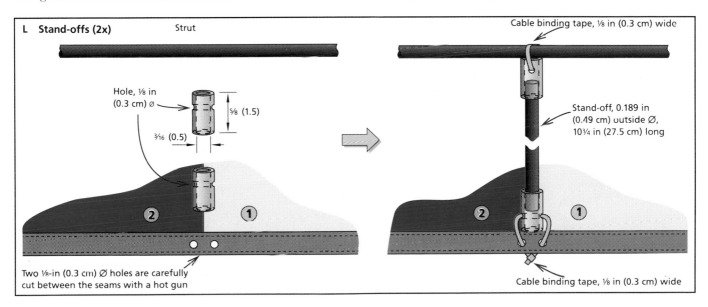

L Stand-offs (2x)

Strut

Cable binding tape, ⅛ in (0.3 cm) wide

Hole, ⅛ in (0.3 cm) ⌀

⅝ (1.5)

3⁄16 (0.5)

② ①

Two ⅛-in (0.3 cm) ⌀ holes are carefully cut between the seams with a hot gun

Stand-off, 0.189 in (0.49 cm) outside ⌀, 10¾ in (27.5 cm) long

② ①

Cable binding tape, ⅛ in (0.3 cm) wide

PARADOX

First and foremost, the Paradox is a four-liner, which means that this kite is steered with four individually attached lines. However, by changing the bridle lines, the kite can also be flown as a so-called one-liner. Do do this, the kite needs an additional tail that will function as a stabilizer. The Paradox is constructed like a box kite and, for that reason, you need a little more wind than necessary to fly a typical flat kite. The speed this kite reaches is moderate, but precise steering is one of its great features. Seven cell-shaped sails provide lift, and the graphite rods used for the frame assure its light weight. In contrast to two-liners, the four-liner is not maneuvered by shifting the air pressure away from the center. Rather, the left and right halves of the sail are steered by two separate lines. By changing angles of inclination, the lift is either reduced or increased:

1. When both sails are level, the kite will rise vertically.
2. When the angle of inclination of both sails is increased, the kite will dip.
3. When both sails are turned against each other, the kite will turn.

This kite is flown with four lines, each 12 inches (30 cm) long and able to bear 175 pounds (80 kg) of pulling power.

Note: Take precautions when working with graphite and fibreglass-reinforced rods or hot-cutting sailcloth, which can be hazardous; use protective goggles, gloves, and a filter mask.

Building Material

2½ sq yd (2 m²) various color nylon sailcloth, 1⁹⁄₁₆ oz/sq yd (52 g/m²)

2½ sq yd (2 m²) cardboard or plywood

2 graphite rods, 44 in (110 cm) long, 0.234 in (0.59 cm) ∅, for side bars

2 graphite rods, 32½ in (82.5 cm) long, 0.234 in (0.59 cm) ∅, for rear struts

4 graphite rods, 13 in (33 cm) long, 0.189 in (0.49 cm) ∅, for center rod

4 graphite rods, 17 inches (43.5 cm) long, 0.182 in (0.48 cm) ∅, for front struts

Pattern Diagram (partially in perspective)

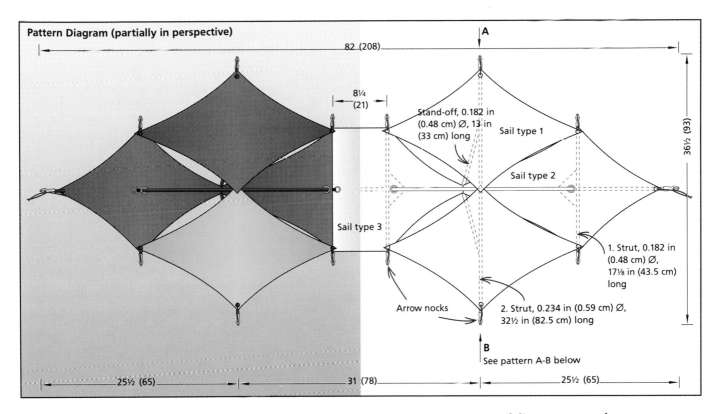

- 82 (208)
- 8¼ (21)
- Stand-off, 0.182 in (0.48 cm) Ø, 13 in (33 cm) long
- Sail type 1
- Sail type 2
- Sail type 3
- 36½ (93)
- 1. Strut, 0.182 in (0.48 cm) Ø, 17⅛ in (43.5 cm) long
- Arrow nocks
- 2. Strut, 0.234 in (0.59 cm) Ø, 32½ in (82.5 cm) long
- A
- B
- See pattern A-B below
- 25½ (65)
- 31 (78)
- 25½ (65)

6 long arrow nocks, ¼ in (0.6 cm) Ø
12 long arrow nocks, ³⁄₁₆ in (0.5 cm) Ø
Dacron material, for reinforcement
14 grommets, ³⁄₁₆ in (0.5 cm) Ø
4 grommets, ⅜ in (1 cm) Ø
1 rubber band, 8 in (20 cm) long, ⅛ in (0.3 cm) Ø, or O-ring
1 rubber band, 40 in (100 cm) long, ¹⁄₁₆ in (0.2 cm) Ø, or O-ring
1 binding tape, 8 in (20 cm) long, ³⁄₁₆ in (0.5 cm) wide
1 binding tape, 12 in (30 cm) long, ⅜ in (1 cm) wide
1 aluminum tube connector, 0.237 in (0.6 cm) inside Ø
1 hose, 8 in (20 cm) long, ³⁄₁₆ in (0.5 cm) inside Ø
1 bridle line, ⅝ in (1.5 cm) Ø
8 aluminum rings, ⅝ in (1.5 cm) Ø

Building Instructions

It is important to read the instructions completely before starting to build this kite. The individual sections of the kite need to be pulled taut, which means it is necessary to provide a series of reinforcements. Techniques used here can also be used later in other box kite constructions. Buy a grommet tool in a spe-

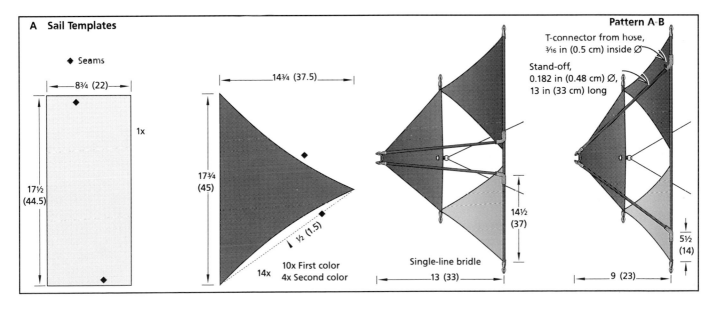

A Sail Templates

Pattern A-B

- ◆ Seams
- 8¾ (22)
- 1x
- 17½ (44.5)
- 14¾ (37.5)
- 17¾ (45)
- ½ (1.5)
- 14x
- 10x First color
- 4x Second color
- Single-line bridle
- 13 (33)
- 14½ (37)
- T-connector from hose, ³⁄₁₆ in (0.5 cm) inside Ø
- Stand-off, 0.182 in (0.48 cm) Ø, 13 in (33 cm) long
- 5½ (14)
- 9 (23)

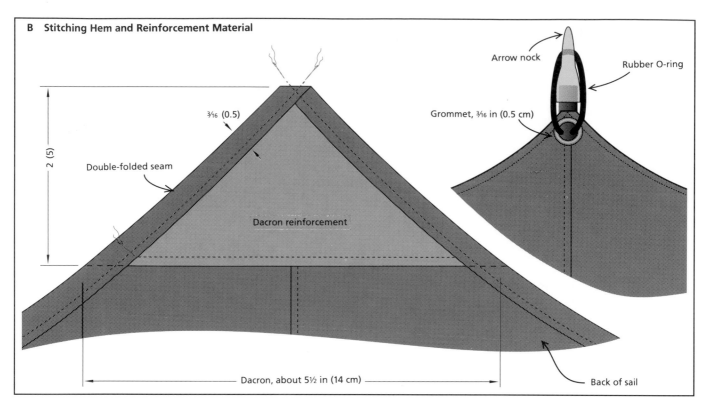

B Stitching Hem and Reinforcement Material

³⁄₁₆ (0.5)

2 (5)

Double-folded seam

Dacron reinforcement

Dacron, about 5½ in (14 cm)

Arrow nock

Rubber O-ring

Grommet, ³⁄₁₆ in (0.5 cm)

Back of sail

cialty store and pay special attention to its quality. The kite consists of two different types of sails. The triangular sail with its concave sides must be cut out 14 times, the rectangular sail only once.

Make sure that you choose a contrasting color for the two sails in the back. Otherwise you will lose the orientation when the kite makes turns during flight. In any case, you must use the hot-cut method when cutting out the sections. That is why we recommend making templates before you start; it makes your job easier.

The triangle shapes, when joined, make six rhombus-shaped sections: four from color #1, and two from the color #2 (see pattern diagram). First, join eight sections (section 1, sketch C), using French seams. Reinforce the corners of the sections with Dacron of the same color (C1). Stitch the 2⅜ by 2¾-inch (6 × 7 cm) triangles and the 2 by 5½-inch (5 × 14 cm) triangles to the back of the sail. For the hem, make sure that ⅜ inch (1 cm) of nylon sailcloth remains (B). We recommend that the

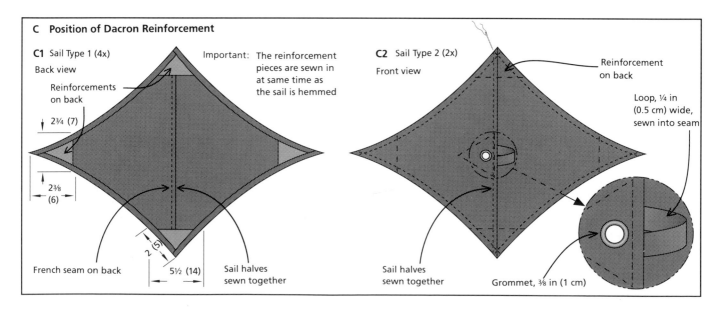

C Position of Dacron Reinforcement

C1 Sail Type 1 (4x)
Back view

Reinforcements on back

2¾ (7)

2⅜ (6)

Important: The reinforcement pieces are sewn in at same time as the sail is hemmed

French seam on back

2 (5)

5½ (14)

Sail halves sewn together

C2 Sail Type 2 (2x)
Front view

Reinforcement on back

Loop, ¼ in (0.5 cm) wide, sewn into seam

Sail halves sewn together

Grommet, ⅜ in (1 cm)

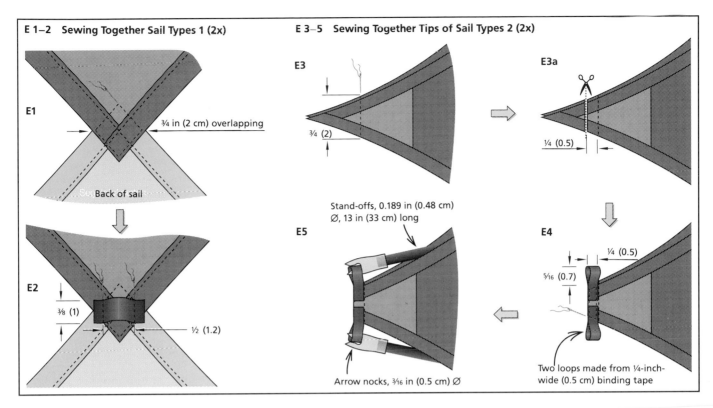

E 1–2 Sewing Together Sail Types 1 (2x)

E1

¾ in (2 cm) overlapping

Back of sail

E2

⅜ (1)

½ (1.2)

E 3–5 Sewing Together Tips of Sail Types 2 (2x)

E3

¾ (2)

E3a

¼ (0.5)

E5

Stand-offs, 0.189 in (0.48 cm)
Ø, 13 in (33 cm) long

Arrow nocks, ³⁄₁₆ in (0.5 cm) Ø

E4

¼ (0.5)

⁵⁄₁₆ (0.7)

Two loops made from ¼-inch-
wide (0.5 cm) binding tape

---

sail reinforcement and the hems are stitched together at the same time: place the Dacron on top of the nylon, double-fold the hem, and sew them together simultaneously. All other Dacron reinforcements and hems, however, must be sewn according to the following instructions: always stitch the reinforcement in place first, and then make the hem of the two sewn-together halves.

Sail type 2 must be sewn twice (C2). Both are later attached on the left and the right of the kite. As a rule these sails are sewn just like the type 1 sail, except that you add a loop in the middle of the French seam which will be at the front side of the sail. Place a ⅝-inch (1.5 cm)

Ø aluminum ring into the loop when you sew it. On the back of this type of sail, stitch a triangular piece of Dacron, using the same color, for reinforcement (C2). Now proceed as you did for type 1. Sail type 3 is made only once; see diagram D, which says that you must join two triangular sections to the rectangular sail. Halfway down the seam, you must again insert one loop each, with an aluminum ring, on the front of the sail. Also, two pieces of Dacron are sewn to the back as reinforcements. Next, stitch together two different colors of the same type-1 sails. This step has to be carried out very carefully, otherwise the symmetry of the whole kite could be compromised. Fold the tips of the kite over ¾ inch (2 cm) and stitch them together, with the seam forming a square (E2). On the back of the sail, sew a small loop to the tip (E2).

Now, a type 2 sail is sewn to the tip of 3 sail. The tips are overlapping by ¾ inch (2 cm) and secured by stitching several times back and forth. The tips are removed with a hot knife. Diagrams E3 and E4 illustrate how a ¼-inch-wide (0.5 cm) binding tape is stitched to the seam, creating two loops which later

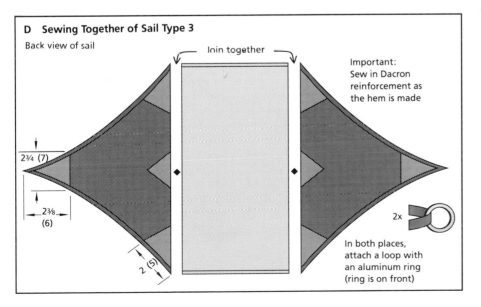

D Sewing Together of Sail Type 3
Back view of sail

Join together

Important:
Sew in Dacron
reinforcement as
the hem is made

2¾ (7)

2⅜ (6)

2 (5)

2x

In both places,
attach a loop with
an aluminum ring
(ring is on front)

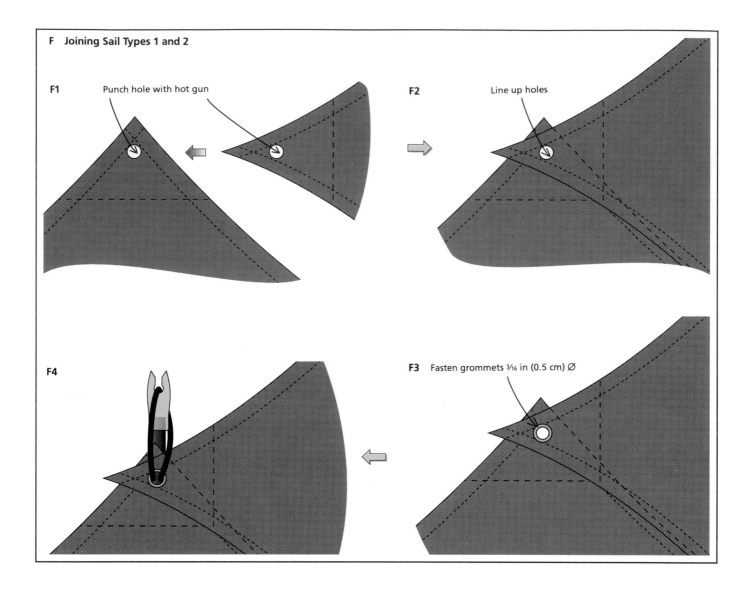

F   Joining Sail Types 1 and 2

F1   Punch hole with hot gun

F2   Line up holes

F4

F3   Fasten grommets ³⁄₁₆ in (0.5 cm) Ø

accommodate the nocks for the stand-offs (E5). The binding tape must be secured in place by stitching back and forth several times. Sewing is now completed. Check all seams again, making sure that they are able to withstand the considerable tension placed on them later.

The next step is to join the individual pieces together using ³⁄₁₆-inch (.05 cm) Ø grommets. With a hot gun, punch ³⁄₁₆-inch (0.5 cm) Ø holes in the tips of the sections that are to be joined together. The holes, as shown in diagram F1, are placed at an acute angle. Push a grommet through both holes of the joining sections. Now, fasten the grommets together using the grommet

tool and a washer on the back of the sail (F1).

First attach two sails each of the type 1 to the outer sails type 2 (four grommets). Make sure that the rivets are tight and secure. Also, make sure that the sections are at a right angle to each other. Next, place the opposite tip of the sails type 1 over the corners of type 3 according to diagrams H1 and 2. Again, the tips of type 1 are on top of the corners of type 3. Tighten all four grommets with the grommet tool and insert graphite rods.

First, insert the four short struts, 0.182 inch (0.48 cm) Ø and 17½ inches (43.5 cm) long. Place the appropriate arrow nocks over the end of the struts.

Diagram F4 shows how the sail is tightened with a rubber band. The two struts, 0.234 inch (0.59 cm) Ø and 32½ inches (82.5 cm) long, do not need to be cut. These are standard lengths that are easily available on the market. Slide the rods through the loops. In front and behind the loops, place T-connectors made from pieces of hose ³⁄₁₆ inch (0.5 cm) inside Ø; see pattern diagram. With the help of arrow nocks and rubber bands, the sail are tightened over the struts.

One strut 80 inches (220 cm) long, 0.234 inch (0.59 cm) Ø, tightens the whole sail of the kite. This rod consists of two pieces joined together with an aluminum tube 0.237 inch (0.6 cm) in-

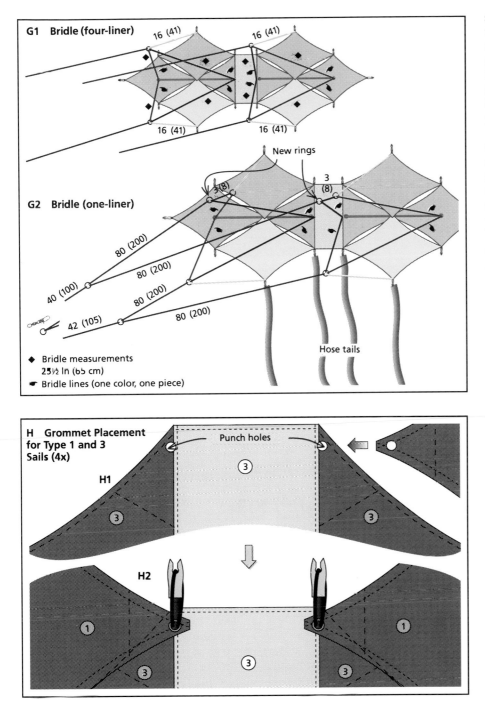

G1 Bridle (four-liner)

16 (41) 16 (41)

16 (41) 16 (41)

New rings

G2 Bridle (one-liner)

3 (8) 3 (8)

80 (200)

80 (200)

40 (100)

80 (200)

42 (105) 80 (200)

Hose tails

◆ Bridle measurements
25½ In (65 cm)

✎ Bridle lines (one color, one piece)

H Grommet Placement for Type 1 and 3 Sails (4x)

Punch holes

H1

③ ③

③

H2

① ①

③

③ ③

side ⌀. Fasten both ends of the rod into the tube with fast-acting glue. Provide sail types 2 and 3 with ⅜-inch (1 cm) ⌀ grommets where reinforcement has been sewed on. Make the appropriate-size hole with a hot gun. You might have to remove the struts for this procedure.

Next, slide the 80-inch (220 cm) struts through the grommets. On sail type 3, the rod lies behind the short strut, while on type 2, it goes in front of the short strut. Attach the appropriate arrow nocks to the ends of the rods, which are held in place with rubber bands. The final stretching of the sail is done with the aid of 13-inch (33 cm) stand-offs (see pattern diagram). About 5½ inches (14 cm) away from the arrow nocks, the T-connectors are held in place by sticky tape. Depending on the version you are building, the measurement may vary. Place the stand-offs in proper loops and connectors.

The kite is now completely assembled and ready for the bridle. Follow the instructions on diagram G1. Cut the bridle line so it is attached to the rings with only one loop. Four aluminum rings hold the steering line in place.

Someone discovered that this kite can also be flown as a one-liner. To do this, only a few small bridle adjustments need to be made. Four pieces of tail hose, as shown in the photo on page 50, must be attached (see diagram G2 for directions). In addition to the original upper-bridle rings, two more aluminum rings are added 3 inches (8 cm) apart. The 71-yard-long (65 m) bridle leg is looped through these rings. A front-connecting bridle 40 inches (100 cm) long, and a rear-connecting bridle 42 inches (105 cm) long, run through the single ring to which the flying line is attached.

One-Line Kites

SAMURAI

Every kite flier dreams of having a kite that can be flown regardless of wind condition. However, such a kite has yet to be realized. To avoid frustration, and so as not go home without being able to fly your kite, you should always arrange to have several different kites on hand: V-shaped kites for medium winds, and flat kites for light winds. The Genki, built by Nop Velthuizen of Holland, served as the basis for this next kite. What is amazing about it is its wing span: 130 inches (325 cm), or over ten feet! With its flat sails and lightweight frame made from graphite rods, the Samurai is the perfect light-wind flyer. We did change the design slightly from

the one in the photo. The most obvious changes are the visual aspects, which give the face more character. The photo above is only provided as an example of the effect that can be achieved with relatively little effort. The sail surface is ideal for attaching an appliqué design. See pages 4 to 6 for inspiration. The fringes, implying a bird, are mostly decorative and are not needed or meant to stabilize the kite. You can easily do away with them if you prefer a different design. The kite should be flown with a line that can tolerate 175 pounds (80 kg) of pull.

Note: Avoid inhaling dust and/or vapors when working with graphite

and fibreglass-reinforced materials, or while cutting sailcloth with a hot-knife or soldering gun.

Building Material

4¾ sq yd (4 m²) nylon sailcloth, 1 oz/sq yd (32 g/m²)
3 graphite rods, 30 in (76 cm) long, 0.182 in (0.48 cm) ∅
2 aluminum tubes, 0.197 in (0.5 cm) inside ∅
2 graphite rods, 32½ in (82.5 cm) long, 0.234 in (0.59 cm) ∅
2 graphite rods, hollow, 32½ in (82.5 cm) long, 0.296 in (0.75 cm) inside ∅, 0.351 (0.89 cm) outside ∅

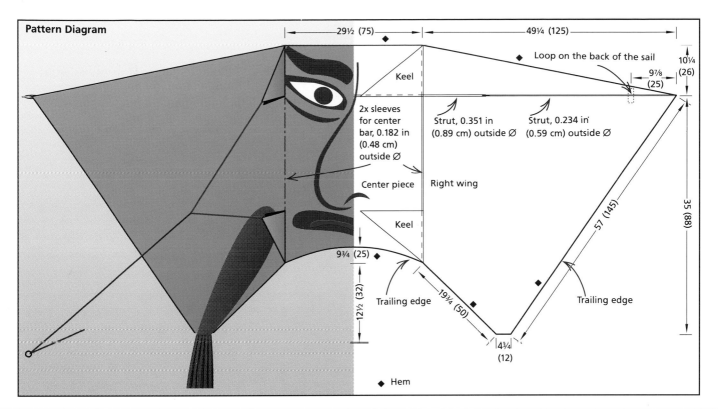

Pattern Diagram

29½ (75) | 49¼ (125)

Keel

◆ Loop on the back of the sail

10¼ (26)

9⅞ (25)

2x sleeves for center bar, 0.182 in (0.48 cm) outside ∅

Strut, 0.351 in (0.89 cm) outside ∅

Strut, 0.234 in (0.59 cm) outside ∅

Center piece

Right wing

Keel

57 (145)

35 (88)

9¾ (25) ◆

12½ (32)

Trailing edge

19¾ (50)

Trailing edge

4¾ (12)

◆ Hem

---

3 aluminum sleeves, 4¾ in (12 cm) long, 0.237 in (0.6 cm) inside ∅, 0.296 in (0.75 cm) outside ∅
1 graphite sleeve, 2¾ in (7 cm) long, 0.296 in (0.75 cm) inside ∅
1 rubber band, 8 in (20 cm) long, ⅛ in (0.3 cm) ∅
3 aluminum rings, ¾ in (2 cm) ∅

Building Instructions

Before buying the material, read the instructions from beginning to end! For the struts you have the choice of either using fishing rod tubes or graphite rods. The frame for the kite discussed here was made with graphite rods. Some of the rods come in standard sizes. If the rods you are buying

are all made by the same manufacturer, they will generally fit together very well; this would eliminate the use of connectors, such as those illustrated here. It's best to seek the advice of an expert.

Essentially, the Samurai consists of three sections: one center section and two side sections. The side sections, again, consist of two sections. First, cut

---

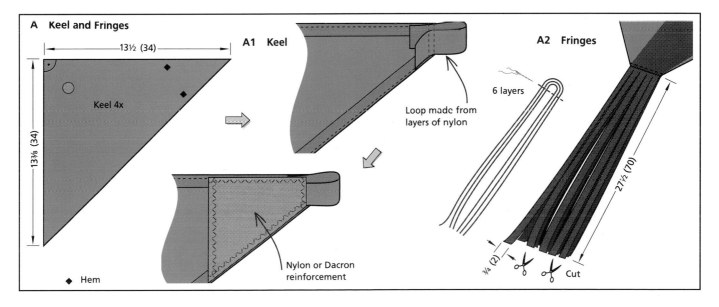

A Keel and Fringes

13½ (34)

A1 Keel

13⅜ (34)

Keel 4x

Loop made from layers of nylon

A2 Fringes

6 layers

27½ (70)

Nylon or Dacron reinforcement

¾ (2)

Cut

◆ Hem

57

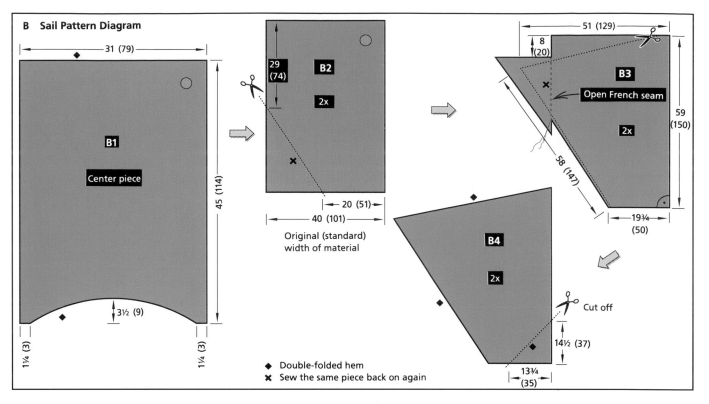

out the center piece according to diagram B1. Two 59-inch-long (150 cm) pieces of nylon, standard 40 inches (101 cm) wide, are cut out and the edges identified in the diagram are cut off (B2). These corners are sewn back with a French seam (B3). Make sure that the seams are on the back.

Excess material is cut off with scissors. Measurements are (see B3): 20 inches (50 cm); 69 inches (150 cm); and 51 inches (129 cm). Furthermore, one part of nylon each is cut off at right angle (B4). Double-folded hems are identified in the pattern diagram by a rhombus. Hems are always in the back. Hem both ends of the center section, on the side pieces three sides. Next, cut out four triangles according to diagram A1. Double-folded hems are identified in the sketch by a rhombus. These are the keels and are later sewn into the center bar sleeves. A loop, consisting of six layers of ripstop nylon, is sewn to both tips of the triangle. Lastly, cut out proper-sized triangles from self-adhesive nylon. They serve as reinforcements and are sewn with zigzag stitches over the hems and over the loops of the triangle (A1). In diagram

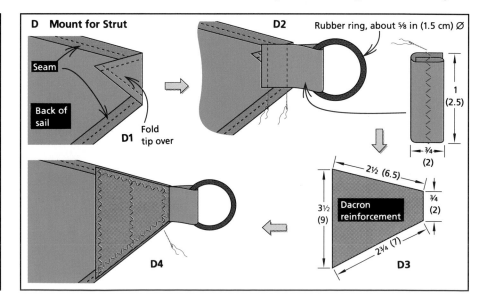

58

E Preparing the Center Bar Sleeves (2x)

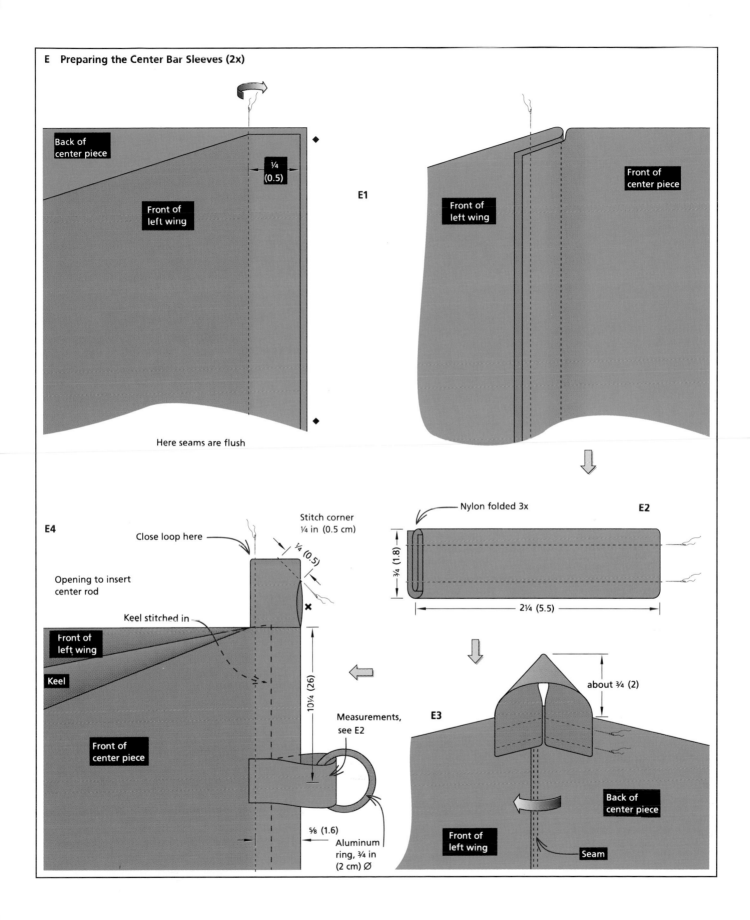

E1

Back of center piece

Front of left wing

¼ (0.5)

Here seams are flush

Front of left wing

Front of center piece

E2

Nylon folded 3x

¾ (1.8)

2¼ (5.5)

E3

about ¾ (2)

Back of center piece

Front of left wing

Seam

E4

Stitch corner ¼ in (0.5 cm)

Close loop here

¼ (0.5)

Opening to insert center rod

×

Keel stitched in

Front of left wing

Keel

Front of center piece

10¼ (26)

Measurements, see E2

⅝ (1.6)

Aluminum ring, ¾ in (2 cm) Ø

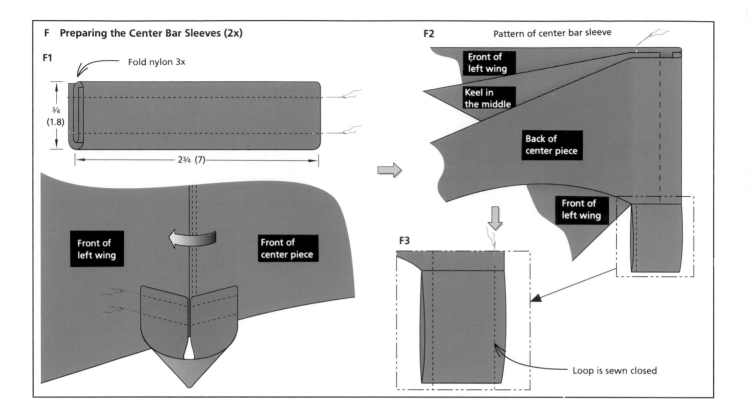

F Preparing the Center Bar Sleeves (2x)

F1
Fold nylon 3x

¾ (1.8)

2¾ (7)

Front of left wing

Front of center piece

F2 Pattern of center bar sleeve

Front of left wing

Keel in the middle

Back of center piece

Front of left wing

F3

Loop is sewn closed

C1, you will notice that small loops made from nylon are sewn onto the seams at the edges. These loops will later hold the strut. Several layers of nylon sailcloth are stitched together with a zigzag stitch into two strips and sewn at the back directly to the French seam, 2 inches (5 cm) apart (diagram C). Loops also have to be sewn on the tips of the side pieces. Prepare the loops as shown in diagram C. The tips of the side pieces are folded back (D1), a rubber O-ring is placed in the loop (D2), and then stitched into place over the fold. The width of the loop must be identical to that of the folded edge. Offset the ends of the loop so that the top extends slightly beyond the edge of the end of the loop underneath. Since these loops are subjected to a lot of stress, they are reinforced with self-adhesive nylon or Dacron the same way the tips of the keel were reinforced, securing the material with the zigzag stitch. The measurements for the proper size are found in diagram D3. Elastic cord can be substituted for the O-ring.

Preparing the center rod sleeve is somewhat more complicated. Study diagrams E1 and E2 carefully before sewing the individual pieces together. First, make two loops as shown in diagram E2. Next, the two wings are sewn to the middle piece (E1), with the seams on the front and using the open-seam method. Make sure that the hem of the trailing edge sits flush against and is sewn into the front edge. Both loops become pockets which will later hold the graphite rods. They are sewn to the front, as shown in diagram E3, as follows: one end of the loop is sewn to the front of the middle piece and the other end to the front of the wing. Next, fold the middle piece over the wing. The fold must be exactly at the vertical seam. Now, place a keel into the sleeve between the middle and the side piece, as shown in the diagram. The keel should be inserted ⅜ inch (1 cm) deep and secured with pins. A second loop, including the ¾-inch (2 cm) ⌀ aluminum ring, is placed on the outside over the sleeve and stitched in place along with the seam. The position is shown in

diagram E4. To make sure that the loop is securely in place, stitch over this seam several times. The aluminum rings are used later for the struts.

The next step is to attach the second keel at the bottom. Position the keel following the pattern diagram. Again, make sure that the hems of the trailing edges are flush. Diagrams F1 through F3 give detailed instructions on how to proceed.

First, make a 2¾-inch-long (7 cm) loop and stitch it to the front. Stitch all the way to the end, which will close the loop (F2). Diagram F3 shows that the loop is entirely closed with a single seam. If you like, you might want to sew fringes to the trailing edges at the sides. This second seam would be stitched along the exact edge of the sleeves. The front loop is closed by stitching across the corner. This creates a pocket that prevents the rod from slipping out (A2).

The vertical rods of the frame consist of 1.5 graphite rods, 30 inches (76 cm) long, 0.182 inch (0.48 cm) ⌀. Cut the rods to size and connect them with

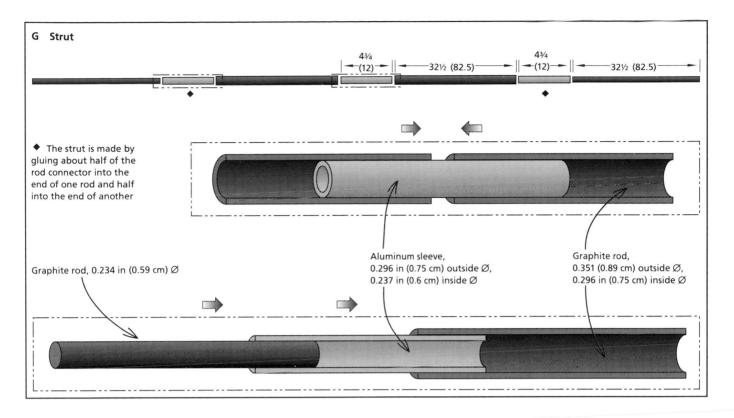

G Strut

4¾ (12) 32½ (82.5) 4¾ (12) 32½ (82.5)

◆ The strut is made by gluing about half of the rod connector into the end of one rod and half into the end of another

Graphite rod, 0.234 in (0.59 cm) ∅

Aluminum sleeve, 0.296 in (0.75 cm) outside ∅, 0.237 in (0.6 cm) inside ∅

Graphite rod, 0.351 (0.89 cm) outside ∅, 0.296 in (0.75 cm) inside ∅

one aluminum connector each 0.197 in (0.5 cm) inside ∅.

The ends of both center rods are covered with vinyl end caps. The rods are placed in the pockets. Struts are made from graphite rods: two are 32½ inches (82.5 cm) long and 0.234 inch (0.59 cm) ∅; two are hollow and 32½ inches (82.5 cm) long and 0.296 inch (0.75 cm) inside ∅. Connect the rods for the appropriate sleeves (G). The connections are fixed in place with fast-acting glue. If you use fishing rod tubes, you need only two. The connections are placed in the middle of the sail. The sail is stretched with the aid of arrow nocks that are attached to the tip of the strut; guide the struts through the loops.

Attach the bridle as shown in diagram H. An overhand knot makes it possible later to change the attack angle. The aluminum ring, ¾ inch (2 cm) ∅, makes balancing the bridle easier.

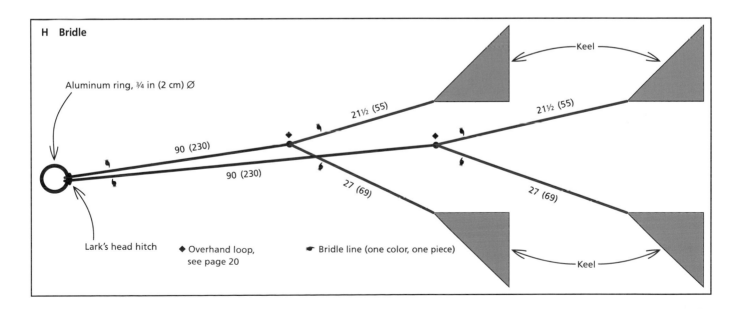

H Bridle

Keel

Aluminum ring, ¾ in (2 cm) ∅

21½ (55) 21½ (55)

90 (230)

90 (230)

27 (69) 27 (69)

Keel

Lark's head hitch

◆ Overhand loop, see page 20

☞ Bridle line (one color, one piece)

STARFLAKE

Facet kites are a relatively new invention, considering how long people have been building kites. But box kites were already being built in Europe as early as the end of the nineteenth century. It was towards the end of 1970 that a few kite builders began to develop facet kites that were unique and beautiful. Stephen Robinson was one pioneer. Later, Scott E. Spencer and Nick van Sant constructed a complicated variation of the kite reminiscent of a snowflake. Every kite builder was fascinated by the facet kite. Mauricio Angeletti perfected these kites, with models that became increasingly dashing and bold, and their popularity quickly began to spread around the world.

The instructions that follow present a variation of the original design. In general, facet kites have one center rod. Several rods, arranged around the center rod, stretch the sail by means of sewing together several small cell-shaped sails. One unique feature distinguishes the Starflake from its predecessors: the individual sails, pointing to the outside, are not held in place by counter-tension. Rather, six small lines, arranged diagonally across the corners, fix the sails in place and provide easy sail-tension capabilities.

The cell-like sails are arranged into halves, upper and lower. Altogether, you need to cut out 36 sections. At first glance, this sounds very cumbersome

and complicated. However, constructing the kite is simpler than you might think. The sections are all sewn together the same way and with straight seams.

Note: Avoid inhaling the dust and/or vapors from working on graphite and fibreglass-reinforced rods, or when cutting sailcloth with a hot knife or soldering gun; these materials are hazardous. It is a good idea to wear protective gloves as well as a filter mask.

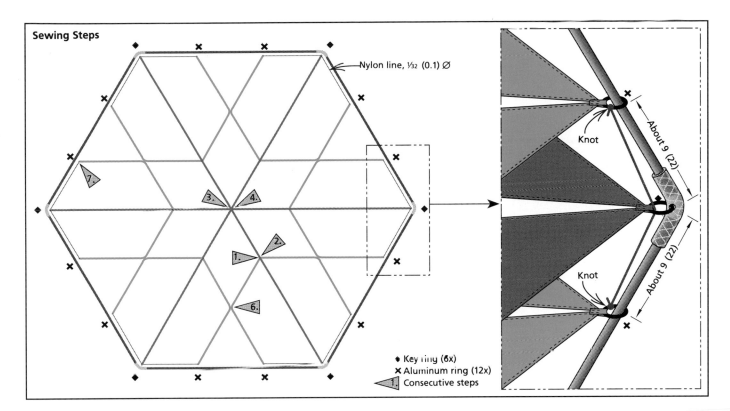

Sewing Steps

Nylon line, ⅟₃₂ (0.1) Ø

Knot

About 9 (22)

About 9 (22)

Knot

◆ Key ring (6x)
✕ Aluminum ring (12x)
◀ 1. Consecutive steps

Building Material

7¼ sq yd (6 m²) turquoise nylon
  sailcloth, 1 oz/sq yd (32 g/m²) fabric
5½ (4.5 m²) neon-pink nylon sailcloth,
  1 oz/sq yd (32 g/m²) fabric
8 graphite rods, 32½ in (82.5 cm) long,
  0.234 in (0.59 cm) Ø
1 aluminum tube, 0.237 in (0.6 cm)
  inside Ø

6 key rings, ¾ in (2 cm) Ø
13 aluminum rings, ⅝ in (1.5 cm) Ø
1 high-pressure hose, 19 in (48 cm)
  long, ¼ in (0.6 cm) inside Ø
1 nylon line, 355 in (900 cm) long
1 binding tape, 80 inches (200 cm) long,
  ⅝ in (1.5 cm) wide
1 nylon cord, 8 in (20 cm) long, ⅟₁₆ in
  (0.2 cm) Ø
2 arrow nocks, ¼ in (0.6 cm) Ø

Building Instructions

The sails are made of two different-
color fabrics: neon-pink and turquoise:
12 sections in pink and 24 in turquoise.
Of course, you may choose whatever
color combination you like; even three
different colors can be used. For the
latter combination, cut out 12 pieces
from each color. Measurements are

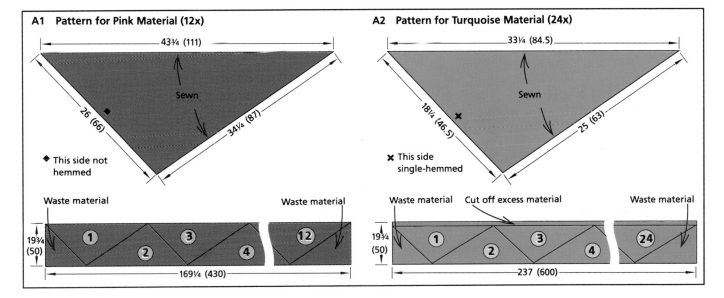

A1 Pattern for Pink Material (12x)

43¾ (111)

Sewn

26 (66)

34¼ (87)

◆ This side not
hemmed

Waste material

Waste material

19¾
(50)

① ② ③ ④

⑫

169¼ (430)

A2 Pattern for Turquoise Material (24x)

33¼ (84.5)

Sewn

18¼ (46.5)

25 (63)

✕ This side
single-hemmed

Waste material

Cut off excess material

Waste material

19¾
(50)

① ② ③ ④

㉔

237 (600)

63

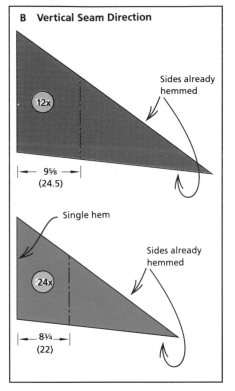

B Vertical Seam Direction

12x

Sides already hemmed

9⅝
(24.5)

Single hem

24x

Sides already hemmed

8¾
(22)

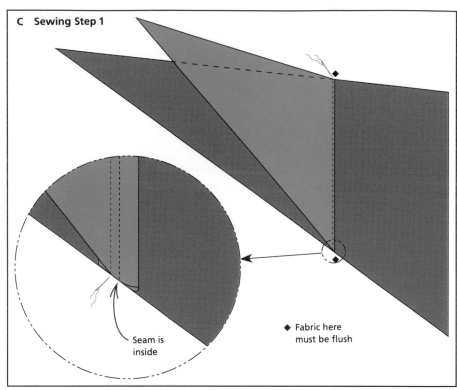

C Sewing Step 1

Seam is inside

◆ Fabric here must be flush

provided in diagrams A1 and A2. One width of material accommodates exactly one large section; when cutting out the 24 smaller pieces you will have a small strip left over. It is best to cut the nylon material with the hot-cutting method. However, since all seams are double-hemmed, you may also use scissors. The pink pieces are hemmed on two sides (see A1). The rhombus-

shaped piece is not hemmed (A1).

All sides of the turquoise-colored pieces have double-folded hems; however, where marked with the cross symbol, use only single-fold hem (A2). Next, mark the direction of the seams on all 36 sections (B) with a soft pencil and a long ruler. Draw a line parallel, as marked, to the edge at a distance of 9⅝ inches (24.5 cm) and 8¾ inches (22 cm)

respectively, as shown. It is very important that these lines and measurements are made with great care. After all 36 sections have been marked, you can start the following sewing steps:

Step 1: One turquoise section is joined on the left and the right by a pink section (C). When folded over, the seams are on the inside. Be very precise when sewing because, if uneven, these

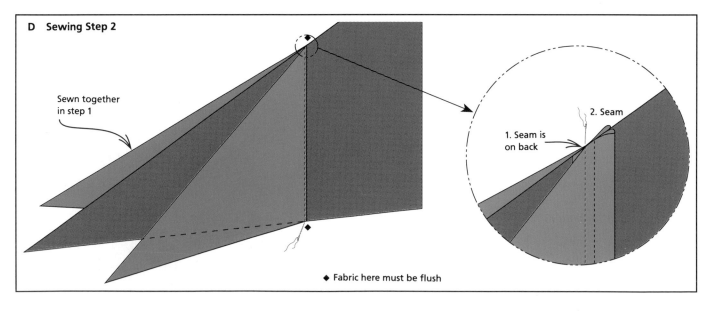

D Sewing Step 2

Sewn together in step 1

2. Seam

1. Seam is on back

◆ Fabric here must be flush

seams can create wrinkles when the sails are stretched. It is very important that the edges of the turquoise and pink fabrics are flush against each other (C). If not, the material will not fold properly along the marked line. Adjust the turquoise fabric along the line until the corners are flush. Step 1 is carried out 12 times.

Step 2: Stitch the same seam on the opposite side of the next turquoise section. The seam should run parallel to the first seam at a distance of 1/16 inch (0.1 cm) (D). This section must also be flush with the edge of the pink sections. Join all 24 pieces in this fashion.

Step 3: Make four stacks of three pink sections each by joining them at the unfinished sides. Stitch the sections together with a single, straight seam 1/8 inch (0.3 cm) away from the edge (E). This step is carried out 4 times.

Step 4: Two of the sections, consisting of three individual pieces, are now joined with a single, straight seam (F1). Make sure that the layers are flush. To be sure, turn the seam over and sew a second seam (F2). You should now have two stacks of sections sewn together.

Step 5: Sew 5/8-inch-wide (1.5 cm) tape directly over each of the seams you made in step 4. The seam is inside when the tape is folded over. Fold the tape at the tip. The loop created in this way is later used to accommodate a so-called tension string (G). The tape on the second stack is only slightly folded

over and the ends are stitched to the tip of the sail. The stack of material must be slightly turned to the inside before stitching the tape in place (G). Now, close the tip of the sleeve of the second stack. The seam on the tip of the first stack remains open (G).

Step 6: Join two turquoise sections together at the line marked previously and as indicated in diagram H. The

edges are placed flush along the line and sewn with a single straight seam; this will avoid wrinkling of the material later on. This step is carried out 12 times.

Step 7: Join together the, up to now still separate, stack of sails. However, before you get started, make 18 loops, 1½ inch (4 cm) long and 5/8 inch (1.5 cm) wide, using three layers of nylon sail-

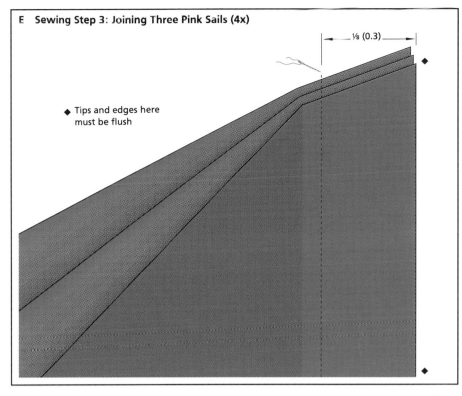

E Sewing Step 3: Joining Three Pink Sails (4x)

1/8 (0.3)

◆ Tips and edges here must be flush

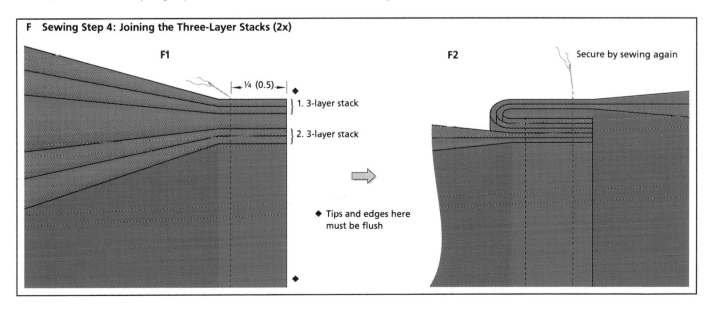

F Sewing Step 4: Joining the Three-Layer Stacks (2x)

F1

1/4 (0.5)

} 1. 3-layer stack

} 2. 3-layer stack

◆ Tips and edges here must be flush

F2

Secure by sewing again

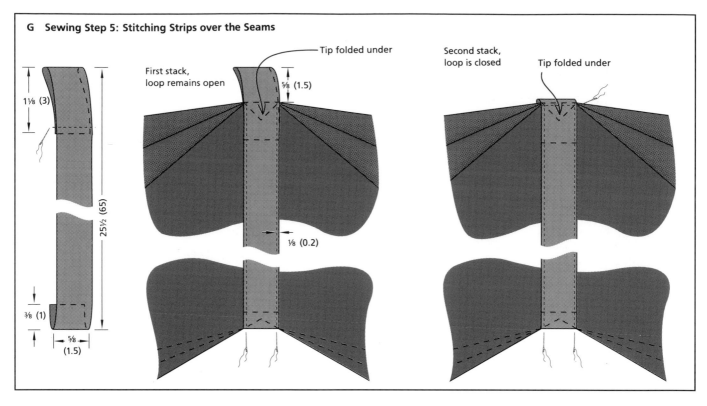

G Sewing Step 5: Stitching Strips over the Seams

1⅛ (3)

25½ (65)

⅜ (1)

⅝ (1.5)

Tip folded under

First stack, loop remains open

⅝ (1.5)

⅛ (0.2)

Second stack, loop is closed

Tip folded under

cloth folded together (12 turquoise, 6 pink). Set aside six key rings ¾ inch (2 cm) ⌀ and twelve aluminum rings ⅝ inch (1.5 cm) ⌀. The following step is repeated 18 times. Place two pink tips on top of each other, according to the instructions in diagram I1, overlapping them by ¾ inch (2 cm). Now, fold over the tip of the two joined sails to a width of ⅝ inch (1.5 cm) (I2). Next, take one

of the triple-layered strips and fold it into a loop, with one of the key rings in place (I3). The loop, extending ⅜ inch (1 cm) beyond the edge, is then stitched to the sail (I4). The aluminum rings, placed into their respective loops, are stitched to the turquoise material; stitch back and forth several times for extra strength, because these points are exposed to a lot of stress when the sails

are stretched. The positioning of the aluminum and key rings is detailed in the diagram on page 63 (top). Sewing is now completed.

Next, cut the high-pressure hose into 3⅛-inch (8 cm) sections. Punch two holes ⅛ in (0.2 cm) ⌀ into the center, opposite each other. Open the key rings and place one into the holes of each piece (K).

Next, insert both center rods. Shorten the 32½-inch (82.5 cm) graphite rod by ⅝ inch (1.5 cm) and slide it into the sleeve that is closed at the tip. The other rod is inserted, without shortening it, into the sleeve with the loop. The two rods are connected with an aluminum sleeve 0.237 in (0.6 cm) inside ⌀. Place an arrow nock over the graphite rod, connecting it to the loop with a nylon cord 1/16 inch (0.2 cm) ⌀. The graphite rod should extend 2 inches (5 cm) beyond its sleeve. Place six graphite rods, 32½ inches (82.5 cm) long, into the holes of the 3⅛-inch (8 cm) lengths of high-pressure hose, while placing two aluminum rings each over the rods. The last rod is used to stretch the sail. If there is too much tension in the sail, shorten the 32½-inch

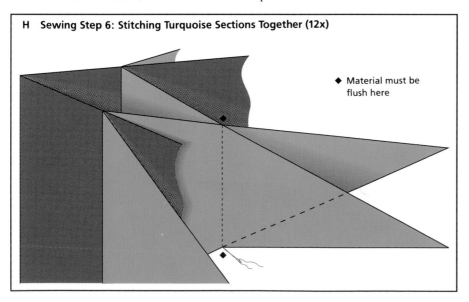

H Sewing Step 6: Stitching Turquoise Sections Together (12x)

◆ Material must be flush here

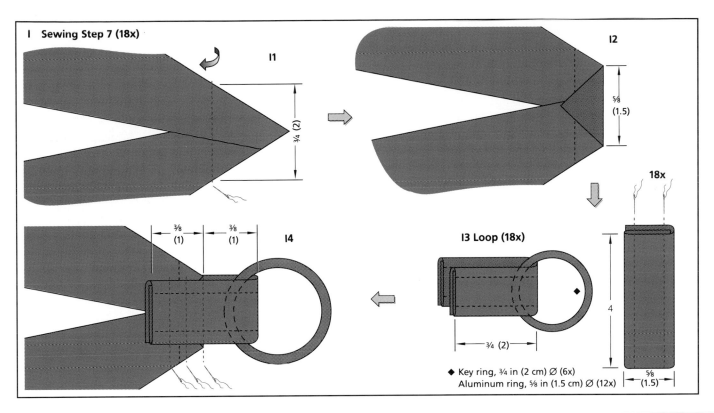

I Sewing Step 7 (18x)

I1

¾ (2)

I2

⅝ (1.5)

18x

I4

⅜ (1)   ⅜ (1)

I3 Loop (18x)

¾ (2)

4

⅝ (1.5)

◆ Key ring, ¾ in (2 cm) ∅ (6x)
Aluminum ring, ⅝ in (1.5 cm) ∅ (12x)

(82.5 cm) graphite rod in small steps and retie the connections. This step-by-step approach works best when tension has to be adjusted.

The turquoise sections to the left and the right of the pink sails are stretched with the nylon line ¹⁄₃₂ inch (0.1 cm) ∅. Carefully tie the nylon line to an aluminum ring. Feed the line through the key ring (K) and tie it to the next aluminum ring (see pattern diagram). Make sure that there is sufficient tension in the turquoise sails. If necessary, take the graphite rods out of the high-pressure hoses during this procedure. The kite has a total of six tension cords, and they are tied into place one section at a time.

The three-legged bridle is attached at the tip and on two hose connectors (see Starflake photo on page 62).

The front length of the bridle is 65⅜ inches (166 cm) long, the rear legs are 70 inches (176 cm) long. If you lengthen the front leg of the bridle by about 8 inches (20 cm) and add an aluminum ring, you will be able to make very precise bridle adjustments any time it becomes necessary.

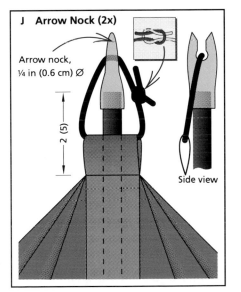

J Arrow Nock (2x)

Arrow nock,
¼ in (0.6 cm) ∅

2 (5)

Side view

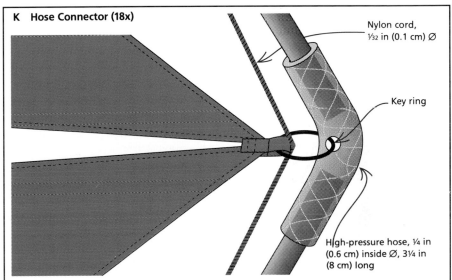

K Hose Connector (18x)

Nylon cord,
¹⁄₃₂ in (0.1 cm) ∅

Key ring

High-pressure hose, ¼ in (0.6 cm) inside ∅, 3¼ in (8 cm) long

STARBIRD

It is the design of the Starbird that makes it so striking. Its sails are a mixture of flat and V-shaped sections. The center is a cross connector made of plastic to which six graphite rods are attached in a star shape. The rear surface of the sail is angled into the wind with a V-shaped cross connector. This surface gives the kite the necessary stability. Both plastic connectors are available in kite shops. Additional stability is provided through 44-inch-long (110 cm) fringe attached in sections to each side of the kite. For transport purposes, the rods that hold the fringes in place are removable through the use of hose connector.

The Starbird is designed for winds between 2.5 and 4 on the Beaufort scale. Experience in using a sewing machine is helpful. Before you start your project read the instructions from beginning to end. This kite is flown with a 175-pound (80 kg) line.

Note: Do not inhale the dust and/or vapors from cutting graphite and fibreglass-reinforced rods, or when hot-cutting sailcloth; take precautions as these materials are hazardous.

Building Material

3 sq yd (2.5 m²) nylon sailcloth,
  1⅜ oz/sq yd (45 g/m²)
3 graphite rods, 30⅛ in (76.5 cm) long,
  0.234 in (0.59 cm) ∅

1 graphite rod, 32½ in (82.5 cm) long,
  0.234 in (0.59 cm) ∅
3 graphite rods, 16⅛ in (41 cm) long,
  0.234 in (0.59 cm) ∅
2 graphite rods, 30⅛ in (76.5 cm) long,
  0.182 in (0.48 cm) ∅
4 fibreglass rods, 9⅞ in (25 cm) long,
  0.079 in (0.2 cm) ∅
1 cross connector, 2–2¼ in (5–6 cm) ∅,
  ⅜ in (1 cm) thick with 8 holes, 0.237
  in (0.6 cm) ∅ (see diagram E)
1 V-connector, 160°, 0.237 in (0.6 cm)
  inside ∅
1 aluminum tube, 2½ in (6.5 cm) long,
  0.237 in (0.6 cm) inside ∅, with center
  bar
1 hard-vinyl hose, 11¾ in (30 cm) long,
  0.237 in (0.6 cm) inside ∅
1 hard-vinyl hose, 2⅜ in (6 cm) long,

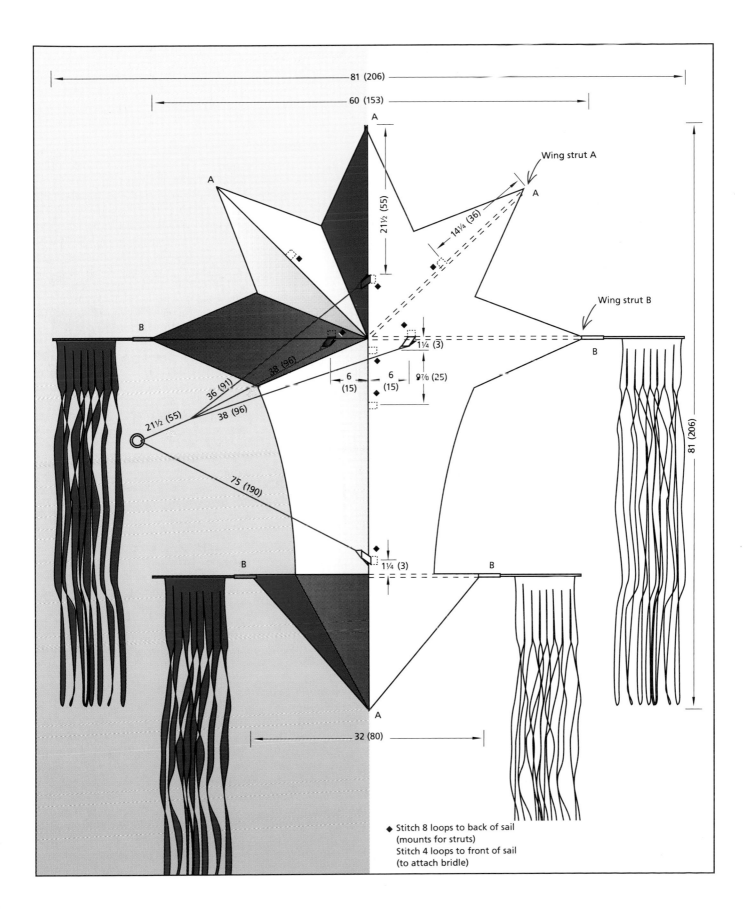

81 (206)

60 (153)

A

A

Wing strut A

A

14¼ (36)

Wing strut B

21½ (55)

B

B

1¼ (3)

38 (96)

36 (91)

6 (15)

6 (15)

9⅞ (25)

38 (96)

21½ (55)

75 (190)

81 (206)

B

B

1¼ (3)

A

32 (80)

◆ Stitch 8 loops to back of sail
(mounts for struts)
Stitch 4 loops to front of sail
(to attach bridle)

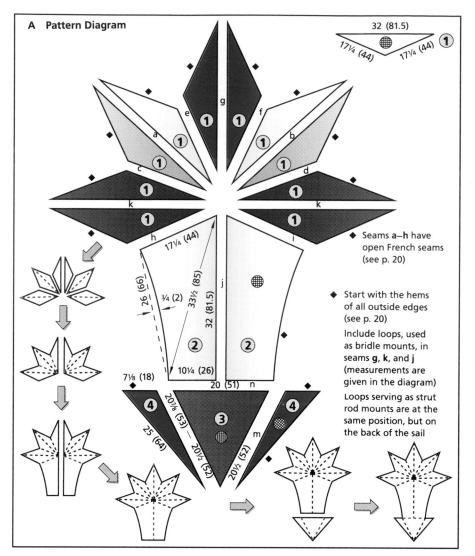

32 (81.5)

17¼ (44)   17¼ (44)   ①

◆ Seams a–h have open French seams (see p. 20)

◆ Start with the hems of all outside edges (see p. 20)

Include loops, used as bridle mounts, in seams **g**, **k**, and **j** (measurements are given in the diagram)

Loops serving as strut rod mounts are at the same position, but on the back of the sail

17¼ (44)
26 (66)
¾ (2)
33½ (85)
32 (81.5)
10¼ (26)
7⅛ (18)
20 (51)   n
20⅛ (53)
25 (64)
20½ (52)
20½ (52)

First, join the pieces marked **a** and **b** (A). You now have a total of four rhombus-shaped pieces. Next, stitch the loops over the seams; they will later hold the struts in place. Each section has one loop. The next step, as illustrated in diagram B, is to stitch one loop each to the side opposite the bridle mounts. The positions of both additional loops are identified in the diagram. Make sure that the loops are securely attached to the sail by stitching back and forth several times.

The color of the loops are the same as the color of the sail to which they are attached.

Next, stitch the seams **c**, **d**, **e**, and **f**. These seams are also on the back. Make sure that, for each seam, the pieces of material are symmetrical and flush.

Now, the sections numbered 2 are sewn to those numbered 1 (seams **i** and **h**; see diagram A). Seams **j** and **g** then join both halves of the large sail. Make sure that the edges of both halves are even and straight. If necessary, use a long piece of wood as a guide to draw a line, and cut off the excess. Remember that two loops are to be included in seam **g** for the bridle mount and the struts. Stitch two loops into seam **j** for the struts and one loop for the bridle mount (see diagram). Make sure that the seams join exactly where the rods of the frames cross each other.

Seams **l** and **m** join both sections of the rear sail, while seam **n** connects the complete rear part to the main sail. One loop each, made from nylon sailcloth, is sewn to the tips (8) of the sail. They are later used for stretching the sail. Instruction on how to make them and attach them to the sail is provided in diagrams C1 to C3. The material is folded and the loops are carefully sewn to the sail. A piece of hose is added to each of four of these tension loops. They are used to stretch the sail (C6). The four outer corners receive a combination of tension loops and mounts for attaching the fringes (see pattern diagram).

Diagrams C4 to C6 indicate that you must first insert a piece of rubber cord into the tension loops. A hole ⅛ inch (0.3 cm) ⌀ is punched into the end of a 1-inch-long (2.5 cm) section of hard-

0.197 in (0.5 cm) inside ⌀
1 hard-vinyl hose, 4¾ in (12 cm) long, 0.237 in (0.6 cm) outside ⌀, 0.157 in (0.4 cm) inside ⌀
1 hard-vinyl hose, 6¼ in (16 cm) long, 0.157 in (0.4 cm) outside ⌀, 0.082 in (0.2 cm) inside ⌀
1 hose, 3¼ in (8 cm) long, ⅛ in (0.3 cm) inside ⌀,
1 elastic cord, 40 in (100 cm) long, ⅛ in (0.3 cm) ⌀
1 nylon line, 20 ft (600 cm) long, ¹⁄₃₂ in (0.1 cm) ⌀
1 aluminum ring, ¾ in (2 cm) ⌀

Building Instructions

The star-shaped front of the kite consists of ten identical sections of nylon cloth. Measurements are given in diagram A. In addition, there are two large middle sections, and three sections make up the rear of the kite. We recommend using the hot-cutting method for all 15 pieces.

To start out, make ¼-inch (0.5 cm) deep, double-folded hems on the outside edges; they are marked with the rhombus symbol in diagram A. Join the star-shaped pieces except for the seam **g** (A) . Loops are sewn into seam **k** (B); they will later accommodate the bridle. You need a total of four loops. Their positions, 6 inches (15 cm) away from the center rod, are identified in the pattern diagram by rhombus symbols. Use French seams and make sure that the seams are on the back.

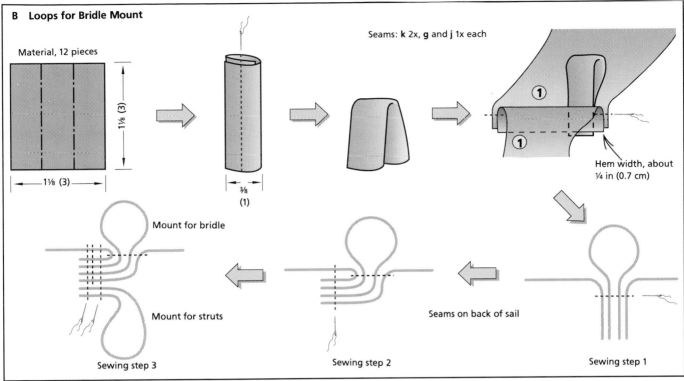

B Loops for Bridle Mount

Material, 12 pieces

1⅛ (3)

1⅛ (3)

⅜ (1)

Seams: **k** 2x, **g** and **j** 1x each

① ①

Hem width, about ¼ in (0.7 cm)

Mount for bridle

Mount for struts

Sewing step 3

Seams on back of sail

Sewing step 2

Sewing step 1

vinyl hose, 0.197 in (0.5 cm) inside ⌀. Guide and then tie the rubber cord through both sides of the hose. The knot must be small enough so that it is able to slip inside the hose. For the thicker graphite rods, 0.234 inch (0.59 cm) ⌀, use hose that has an inside diameter of ¼ inch (0.6 cm); for the thinner graphite rods, 0.182 inch (0.48 cm) ⌀, use hose that has an inside diameter of ³⁄₁₆ inch (0.5 cm). The outer tips on the

left and right side of the kite are provided with tension loops *and* mounts for the ³⁄₃₂-inch (0.2 cm) ⌀ graphite rods. Cut four pieces of hard-vinyl hose according to diagram D1. These pieces are tied to their respective loops according to diagrams C4 to C6. Diagram D2 shows how the loops are attached to the sail.

Next, prepare eight pieces of hard-vinyl hose according to diagram D3:

four 1-inch (2.5 cm) long, 0.237 inch (0.6 cm) outside ⌀, 0.157 inch (0.4 cm) inside ⌀; four ¾-inch (2 cm) long, 0.157 inch (0.4 cm) outside ⌀, 0.082 inch (0.2 cm) inside ⌀. These pieces of hose are attached to the tension rods and, if necessary, glued in place with fast-acting glue (D4).

Diagram E shows the position of the struts as well as their measurements. Cut the rods to their respective length,

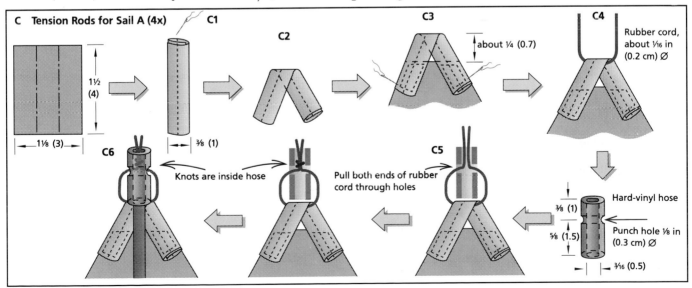

C Tension Rods for Sail A (4x)   C1   C2   C3   C4

1½ (4)

1⅛ (3)

⅜ (1)

about ¼ (0.7)

Rubber cord, about ¹⁄₁₆ in (0.2 cm) ⌀

C6   Knots are inside hose   C5   Pull both ends of rubber cord through holes

Hard-vinyl hose

⅜ (1)

⅝ (1.5)

Punch hole ⅛ in (0.3 cm) ⌀

³⁄₁₆ (0.5)

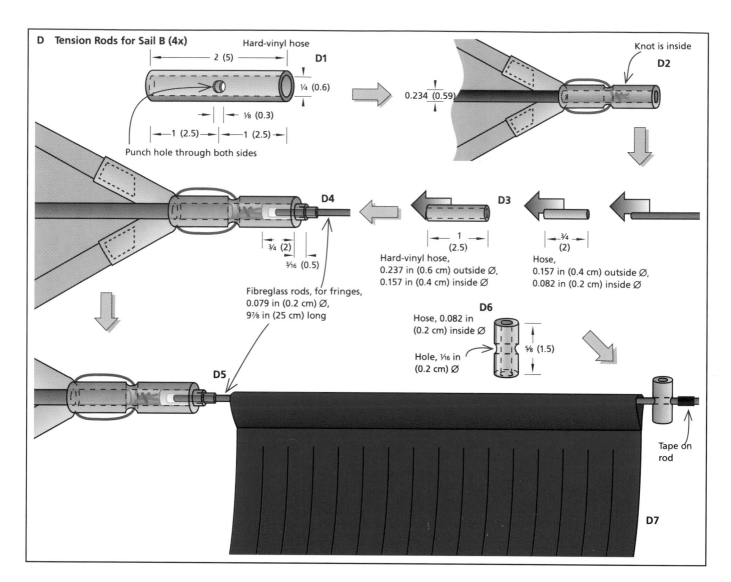

D Tension Rods for Sail B (4x)

Hard-vinyl hose

2 (5)   **D1**

¼ (0.6)

⅛ (0.3)

1 (2.5)   1 (2.5)

Punch hole through both sides

Knot is inside   **D2**

0.234 (0.59)

D4

¾ (2)

³⁄₁₆ (0.5)

Fibreglass rods, for fringes,
0.079 in (0.2 cm) Ø,
9⅞ in (25 cm) long

D3

1 (2.5)

Hard-vinyl hose,
0.237 in (0.6 cm) outside Ø,
0.157 in (0.4 cm) inside Ø

¾ (2)

Hose,
0.157 in (0.4 cm) outside Ø,
0.082 in (0.2 cm) inside Ø

D6

Hose, 0.082 in
(0.2 cm) inside Ø

Hole, ¹⁄₁₆ in
(0.2 cm) Ø

⅝ (1.5)

D5

Tape on
rod

D7

always paying attention to the difference in diameters. Cutting has to be done with great care to avoiding splitting the ends. This is easy if the rods are wrapped with tape at the places where they are to be cut. Remove the tape afterwards. It is recommended that the rods be left somewhat longer than needed, as stated in the diagram. Later, when the rods are assembled and the sail is stretched, the rods can be carefully cut down to the proper size.

The heart of the kite is the round-shaped cross connector (E1) made from hard vinyl. Very important are its eight holes, each 0.237 inch (0.6 cm) Ø and 45° apart. This part can be bought in a kite store. However, if you want to make your own, as illustrated in E1, you may leave out the two holes marked with the rhombus symbol. In addition, the holes should only be ³⁄₁₆ inch (0.5 cm) Ø. If you use a store-bought connector, with holes 0.237 inch (0.6 cm) Ø, the two 0.182 inch (0.48 cm) Ø rods that are to be inserted in the holes have to be wrapped with tape to assure a tight fit.

The hard-vinyl disk is ¾ inch (2 cm) thick and 2⅜ inch (6 cm) Ø. The holes are about ¾ inch (2 cm) deep. The 20° V-connector (E2) can also be bought in a kite store. This is a part that is usually used on stunt kites. This connector comes in different sizes and colors.

Next, assemble the kite frame by sliding the rods into their respective loops on the back of the kite. An aluminum sleeve, 0.237 inch (0.6 cm) inside Ø, connects the 32½-inch (82.5 cm) rod with the 16⅛-inch (41 cm) rod. These connectors, which are also available in kite stores, should have a middle bar. This bar can be glued into place on one side with fast-acting glue. The sail is stretched with a rubber cord. At this point, if necessary, adjust the length of the rods. If the V-connector does not stay in place use a bit of tape.

The decorative fringes provide stability for the kite. For each fringe, cut a piece of nylon sailcloth 44 by 8⅝ inches (110 × 22 cm). The color of the fringes should complement or contrast with the colors used for the sails. The ends of the nylon strips are sewn together. Folding and sewing a 2-inch (5 cm) hem along the length makes a sleeve (F). Make a

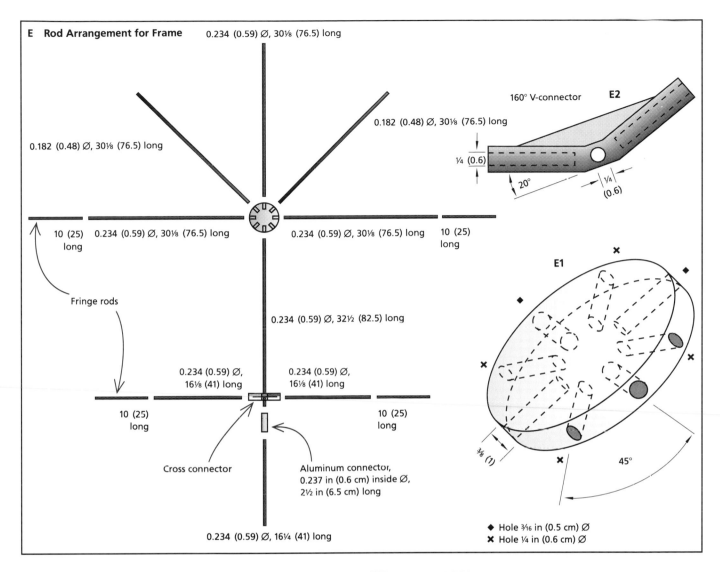

E Rod Arrangement for Frame

0.234 (0.59) Ø, 30⅛ (76.5) long

0.182 (0.48) Ø, 30⅛ (76.5) long

0.182 (0.48) Ø, 30⅛ (76.5) long

160° V-connector

E2

¼ (0.6)

20°

¼ (0.6)

10 (25) long

0.234 (0.59) Ø, 30⅛ (76.5) long

0.234 (0.59) Ø, 30⅛ (76.5) long

10 (25) long

Fringe rods

E1

0.234 (0.59) Ø, 32½ (82.5) long

0.234 (0.59) Ø, 16⅛ (41) long

0.234 (0.59) Ø, 16⅛ (41) long

10 (25) long

10 (25) long

Cross connector

Aluminum connector, 0.237 in (0.6 cm) inside Ø, 2½ in (6.5 cm) long

⅜ (1)

45°

0.234 (0.59) Ø, 16¼ (41) long

◆ Hole 3/16 in (0.5 cm) Ø
✕ Hole ¼ in (0.6 cm) Ø

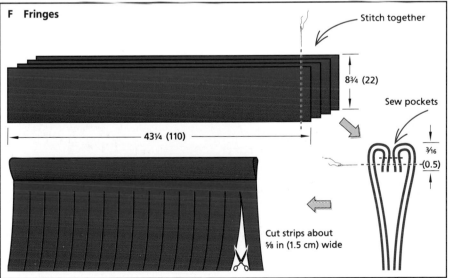

F Fringes

Stitch together

8¾ (22)

Sew pockets

3/16

(0.5)

43¼ (110)

Cut strips about ⅝ in (1.5 cm) wide

total of four pieces and use four fiberglass rods as support.

You need a stopper at the end of the rod to prevent the fringes from sliding off. Punch a hole through the center of a ⅝-inch-long (1.5 cm) piece of hose (D6). Slide this piece over the end of the rod and wrap some tape around the end (D7). At the other end of the rod, attach a ¾-inch (2 cm) long, hard-vinyl hose, 0.157 inch (0.4 cm) outside Ø. If necessary, strengthen the rod with a bit of tape so that the piece of hose remains securely in place. Now, slide the fringes over the rod and the rod into the hard-vinyl hose, 0.157 inch (0.4 cm) inside Ø (D5).

Attach the bridle to the front loops according to the pattern diagram.

Tuning Your New Kite

The bridle of every kite, whether you build it yourself or buy it in a store, must be adjusted from time to time. Changes in wind conditions is one reason. I myself have tested, and successfully flown, each kite discussed in this book.

Nevertheless, it might be necessary to tune the bridle due to various influences, such as differences in building material (sailcloth or frame) and different techniques used in sewing hems, seams, and sleeves.

Every bridle needs to be tuned, after the kite has been built, to assure optimum flight behavior. Here are my suggestions for tuning the kites presented in this book:

One-Liners

If the front leg(s) of a bridle is/are shortened, the kite gains more lift. If your kite still does not gain height or swerves sideways immediately after launch, even with sufficient wind, flatten the flight angle by either shortening the front leg or lengthening the rear leg of the bridle. If the angle of flight is too flat, the kite will sail high above the flier and be very unstable. The kite may even make unintentional loops. If this happens, the flight angle has to be increased: the front leg lengthened or the rear leg shortened.

It is possible for a kite, with the bridle adjusted for minimum wind conditions, to still fly when the wind increases. Most likely, however, it will dance back and forth in the sky; if so, increase the flight angle.

A kite is also unstable when the left and the right side of the bridle are uneven. If the kite pulls to the left, you must shorten the right leg, and vice versa. But do not forget to check the symmetry of the sails, because incorrect flight behavior might result from mistakes made when the pattern was cut out.

If the above steps bring no improvement, check the kite's overall aerodynamic. The wings of flat kites must have a certain V-shape in order to fly properly. This allows the kite to react to the pressure of the air/wind and, with the wings at a slight angle, gives it the necessary stability. A tail or other accessory attached to the trailing edges will provide the kite with additional stability.

Stunt Kites

In general, the rules that apply to single-line kites apply also to stunt kites: If a stunt kite does not gain altitude, shorten the front legs of the bridle; on the other hand, if a kite lifts into the air too fast or crashes after the first maneuver, the rear leg must be shortened and the flight angle increased. If a kite turns big circles in one direction only, only that side needs adjustment: only the front leg of the bridle on that particular side is lengthened. In any case, tuning a bridle is done one millimeter at a time, and only when the wind condition is steady. Similar to single-line kites, stunt kites are also adjusted according to prevailing wind conditions: little wind, the angle is more flat; stronger winds, the angle is steeper. Make small marks on the flying line with a felt-tip pen. Most semi-flexible stunt kites have two points each at the rear of the kites to which the left and the right connecting bridles are attached. These points are marked in the pattern diagram of the Relax II, page 32. Overhand loops are attached here (see page 25). Depending on the situation, these knots/loops can be moved horizontally towards the center or towards the outside. This causes different dispersion of pressure on the sail. If the knots are pushed further to the center, the V-shape of the wings is increased and the kite becomes more stable. This will, however, negatively influence the kite's turning ability. Steering is tighter and the kite tends to oscillate when it makes tight turns. If the knots are pushed further to the outside, the V is flattened and the kite will fly faster. However, tight turns can still be carried out with precision because the distance of the steering line is increased. In any case, changing the position of the knots influences the V-angle of the sails and, for that reason, fine tuning, where appropriate, becomes necessary.

The arch of the Rogallo kite influences the speed and stability of stunt kites. A low arch makes for a fast kite but also decreases stability. If the arch is increased, the kite becomes more stable but will also be slower. Make sure, therefore, that you check the slack in the sail. As we have already discussed, different sewing techniques will influence the slack of the sail. In general, the quotient between the length of the rear side bar and that of the slack of the sail is between 3.5 and 4.5.

The parafoil Paraflex is a totally flexible stunt kite.

Flying Stunt Kites

Aerodynamics

If you want to fly your kite successfully and be able to perform skillful maneuvers, you need to learn a few basic aerodynamic principles.

The pressure that the wind exerts at the front of the kite creates a pressure center at the surface of the sail, to give it maximum lift; this pressure diminishes as the air moves towards the leading edge (see diagram A). In general, two factors influence lift: the wind pressure at the front of the kite and the reduced pressure at the rear (because of the higher wind speed).

The job of the bridle and the steering lines is to counter the overall force created by lift and pull and keep the kite in the air, as well as to determine the kite's angle of attack.

The combined forces make the kite veer to the right if you pull on the right steering line. Kites steer to the right against the wind because, for instance in the launching phase (where the kite rises up), a kite will always attempt to balance the forces that are pulling it (see B and C). The kite makes a circle above the flier, constantly changing its posi-

tion by trying to adjust to the wind. A kite has reached its highest point against the wind when the resulting combined forces are again lined up with the steering lines (see A).

The closer a kite flies to the ground, the more vertical its orientation in relation to the wind. The higher a kite flies against the wind, the more its speed and pulling force are reduced. The same holds true for the vertical flight of a stunt kite: the pulling force is at its lowest when a kite has reached its maximum lift. The higher the kite is in the air, the more speed it looses, until it stands almost motionless in the sky. If, at this particular moment, the kite is steered downwards, its wind resistance constantly increases, which also causes an increase in speed and pulling force.

Launching and Landing

Launching and landing a kite are usually the two most difficult maneuvers for a kite flier. Often, wind turbulence close to the ground or lines and tails that get tangled up with one another can make launching your kite impossible. The

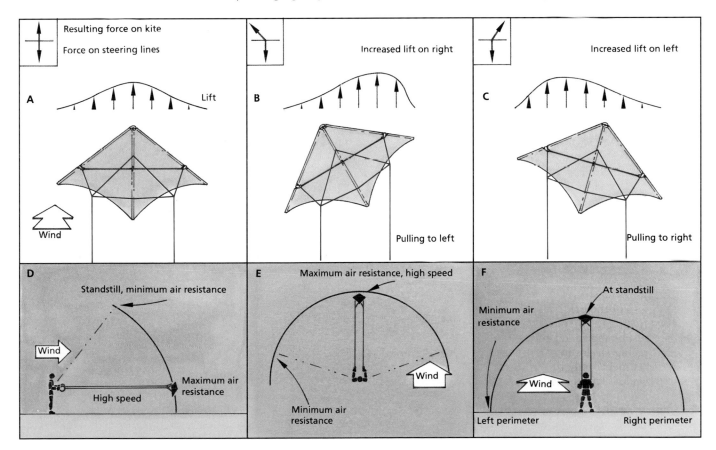

choice of a proper location is very important. Try to avoid places where houses, trees, dams, etc., cut the wind, because there is usually ground turbulence behind such structures that makes a launch difficult. Look for empty airfields, places alongside lakes or shores with the wind blowing out over the water, or large pastures.

Stunt kites can be launched in three ways: from the hand, with the aid of a helper, or by solo ground start.

1. You can hand-launch your kite only if wind conditions are good. First, attach both steering lines to the kite and hold the kite out about a yard, or metre, in front of you. With a sharp, short tug upwards, pull the kite into the air. The wind needs to be brisk enough so that the kite lifts directly overhead and stays there. If that is the case, begin to release both steering lines equally (this technique works best using round reels).

2. A helper, if available, holds the kite high into the wind about 30 yards, or metres, away from you and lets go on your command. Start pulling equally on both steering lines, letting the air pull the kite into the air. If you are flying a kite train with more than three kites, ask your helper to hold the very last kite on the ground, pulling enough so that all kites stand upright.

3. First, lay out about 35 yards or metres of steering line on the ground in a straight line. Connect the line to a reel and anchor the reel in the ground (use two anchors or two small pieces of wood). Only now should you connect the kite to the steering line. Pull on the steering line to up-right your kite against the wind. Kites that have horizontal trailing edges are placed on the ground on their tips. Kites that have trailing edges ending in points are placed on the ground on one of their leading edges or side rods.

It is best to land a maneuverable kite by flying it against the wind and allowing it to descend slowly (see diagram E, page 75—minimal air resistance). The disadvantage of this method is that you won't be able to start your kite again from the point where it will land.

Experienced kite fliers are able to land their maneuverable kite even when high wind resistance exists. They initiate a power dive or let the kite fly horizontally low over the ground as they stand in the center of an airfield. A short tug on the steering line makes the kite lift upwards again into the sky. At the moment when the kite begins to rise, the flier takes a few jogging steps forward; the result is that the kite begins to sink. With a bit of skill, a flier can make the kite land on the trailing edge.

Solo Flying

Watching an experienced stunt-kite flier skillfully and powerfully maneuver a kite close to the ground might convince you that such flying techniques are very hard to learn. However, that is not the case. I myself have seen beginners make right and left turns, as well as perform simple figures,

after only a very short period. As discussed, maneuverable kites will turn right when the flier pulls on the right steering line, and turn left when the left steering line is pulled.

After you have launched your kite into the sky, first try to keep it quietly in the air by pulling alternately on the lines. The ideal situation is one when your kite, flying with the wind, is directly overhead (see diagram F, page 75). Prerequisite is that both steering lines are equal in length and that you pull evenly on both lines. Only after you have mastered the skill of keeping your kite relatively quiet in the air (motionless is never really accomplished) should you begin to practise left and right turns. This is best accomplished when you pull alternately on the steering lines in small pendulum like movements. Just pull a bit on the right steering line. After the kite has moved to the right (about 50 feet, 15 m), hold the right side and at the same time tug on the left steering line. Move your kite in this fashion from left to right, the same way as if you were riding your bike slalomlike from one side to the other. This type of movement is also recommended when you fly a stunt kite with a steering bar (see photos below).

Pulling the right steering line results in a right turn. Pulling the left steering line results in a left turn.

Team Flying

Only those who are experienced solo fliers should get involved in team flying. In team flying the kites fly very close together, and only if one is able to control a stunt kite perfectly (flying circles, turns, making power dives, and flying horizontally) is it possible to prevent mid-air collisions and crashes. Team flying with stunt kites can include two or more people; but before several get involved, they should first work in groups of two or three with one taking the responsibility of leader. The leader is the only one to give the commands.

In general, there are two different methods of team flying:
1. Participating kites are flown parallel to each other, which means that their maneuvers are synchronized.
2. The kites fly closely behind each other (see photo, upper right).

For effective team flying, when several people participate, there must not only be absolute harmony of movement, but one person who acts as coordinator and gives the steering commands (easiest with a megaphone), for instance: "Turn left," "Move right," and "Circle upward." Each individual command is followed with the instruction "*now*," so that all participants will carry out the command at the exact same time.

Stunt-kite teams from the United States often tour Europe and impress everyone with their skills. In team flying, it can happen that, when two or more kites follow each other, lines may cross over each another. This is of little consequence as long as the kites use the same type flying line; otherwise, there is a chance that they might cut each other.

It is important that all participants synchronize their steering maneuvers.

If several kites follow each other, the flier of the first kite gives the commands.

Maneuvers carried out by individual fliers are not affected if their steering lines cross each other, even if more than once.

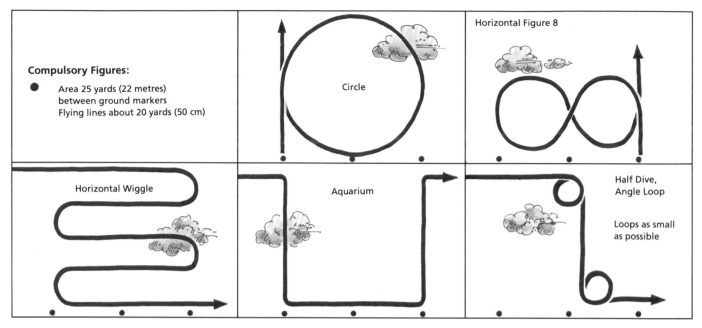

Compulsory Figures:

● Area 25 yards (22 metres) between ground markers Flying lines about 20 yards (50 cm)

Circle

Horizontal Figure 8

Horizontal Wiggle

Aquarium

Half Dive, Angle Loop

Loops as small as possible

Flight Patterns

Some figures that reveal technique and might be compulsory in stunt-kite championships are: "Circle," "Horizontal Figure 8," "Horizontal Wiggle," "Half Dive, Angle Loop," and "Aquarium." They are usually judged as follows:

Circle: A smooth line and true circle.

Horizontal Figure 8: Smooth loops, round and of same size; both loops an equal distance from the ground; a closed figure, meaning that the figure ends at the same point as it started.

Horizontal Wiggle: Horizontal figures run parallel; distance is equal between the loops in the horizontal and vertical planes; the figure is flown from left to right.

Half Dive, Angle Loop: A straight flight path; small loops; vertical center axis; close to the ground after the last loop; starts on the upper right.

Aquarium: Rectangular flight lines with sharp corners, a horizontal plane close to the ground; starts upper left.

Other figures, shown in the diagrams on page 79, are often freestyle in kite competitions.

Every year, the Danish island Fanø hosts the International Kite Flyers Competition. Participants encounter excellent flying conditions on a wide beach that is miles long. It is an occasion and opportunity for many to share their experiences.

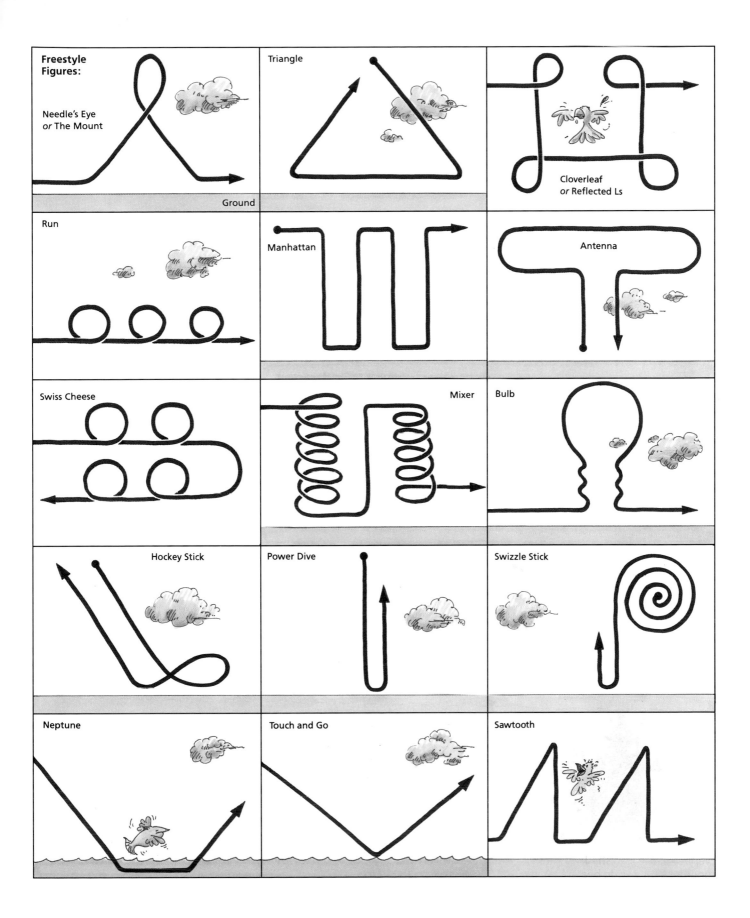

Freestyle Figures:

Needle's Eye *or* The Mount

Ground

Triangle

Cloverleaf *or* Reflected Ls

Run

Manhattan

Antenna

Swiss Cheese

Mixer

Bulb

Hockey Stick

Power Dive

Swizzle Stick

Neptune

Touch and Go

Sawtooth

Kite Safety

In stunt-kite flying, SAFETY is spelled in *capital* letters. The following kite-flying guidelines should be observed at all times:

1. Do not fly your kite in a storm; high winds could cause you to lose control, and a lightning strike could kill you.
2. Flying lines that are stretched thin can cause severe cuts, especially lines made from Kevlar or similar fibre. Wear protective gloves, and watch out for spectators.
3. Do not fly your kite near antennas or power lines (in many places it is against the law); you could be killed. If your kite should get caught on an electric power line, do not touch the line. If the kite doesn't work free, and you won't just walk away, contact the utility company or fire department.
4. Stay away from roads, highways, or other traffic routes so that a kite crash won't cause a car crash. Stay at least 3 miles (5 km) away from active airports.
5. Remember that kites can be dangerous to animal life: horses may bolt, cattle or sheep may panic, disturbed nesting birds might abandon their eggs. Also, stay away from protected wildife areas.
6. Don't fly your kite in quiet recreational areas, where people go to peacefully relax; many kites are noisy and can be disturbing. Never fly your kite low over the heads of people or animals; if they are startled, they could become injured.
7. Don't leave things behind, such as sailcloth scraps, flight lines, or ground anchors. Animals can die from eating such things. Don't walk on tilled fields or tie your kite to a tree; always use a ground anchor, available in kite stores—or you can make them yourself.
8. Very long lines are dangerous; limit your flying lines to about 100 yards or meters.
9. At eye or ground level, attach colored tape to your flying lines, anchors, or other objects so that they are visible and easily noticed.

It is especially important to be alert when launching and landing your kite. Pay attention to other nearby kites, their fliers, and passersby.

Index